01343424

Daggers and Fighting Knives

of the Western World

From the Stone Age till 1900

ARMS AND ARMOUR SERIES

General Editor: CLAUDE BLAIR

Other titles in this Series

REVOLVING ARMS by A. W. F. Taylerson
ORIENTAL ARMOUR by H. Russell Robinson

In preparation:
HUNTING WEAPONS by Howard Blackmore
ITALIAN FIREARMS by James Lavin
ENGLISH PISTOLS, 1650–1750 by F. Wilkinson and A. Littler
ENGLISH ARMOUR by Claude Blair

Daggers and Fighting Knives
of the Western World

From the Stone Age till 1900

by

HAROLD L. PETERSON

68

HERBERT JENKINS
LONDON

© 1968 by Harold L. Peterson

First published 1968 by
Herbert Jenkins Ltd
2 Clement's Inn, London, W.C.2

Made and printed in Great Britain by
W. & J. Mackay & Co Ltd, Chatham, Kent

CONTENTS

LIST OF PLATES

between pages 66 and 67

ACKNOWLEDGEMENTS

The Author and Publishers wish to thank the following for permission to reproduce the illustrations appearing in this book.

Robert Albrecht, for Plate 79

Bernisches Historisches Museum, for Plate 43

William C. Borland, for Plate 6

The Trustees of the British Museum, London, for Plate 7

Herb Glass, for Plate 87

The Guildhall Museum, London, and especially Mr Martin Henig, for Plates 14, 22, 25

John D. Hammer, for Plates 88, 95

Historisches Museum, Basel, for Plate 34

The Master of the Armouries, H.M. Tower of London, for Plate 63 (Ministry of Works, Crown Copyright, reproduced by permission of the Controller of H.M. Stationery Office)

Archer L. Jackson, for Plate 91

Dr John K. Lattimer, for Plates 85, 92, 93

The Metropolitan Museum of Art, New York, for Plates 11, 12 (Gift of George D. Pratt, 1930), 19, 54 (Bashford Dean Memorial Collection Purchase, 1929, Funds from Various Donors), 46, 53 (Rogers Funds, 1904), 31, 32, 33, 36, 37, 38, 39, 40, 52, 61, 73, 74, 75, 76 (Gift of Jean Jacques Reubell, 1926, in memory of his mother Julia C. Coster, and his wife, Adeline E. Post, both of New York City)

Musée d'Art et d'Histoire, Geneva, for Plates 28, 29, 42

The Trustees of the National Maritime Museum, Greenwich, London, for Plates 96, 97, 98, 99, 100, 101, 102, 103, 104

Naturhistorisches Museum, Vienna, for Plates 8, 9

Leonard B. Pelton, for Plate 77

Ben Palmer, for Plates 86, 90

Royal Ontario Museum, Toronto, for Plate 1

Schweizerisches Landesmuseum, Zürich, for Plates 10, 21, 23, 24, 26, 27

Scottish United Services Museum, Edinburgh Castle, for Plates 70, 71, 72

James E. Serven, for Plate 83

Statens Historiska Museum, Stockholm, for Plates 2, 3

Norman Tapley, for Plate 84

U.S. National Museum, Smithsonian Institution, Washington, for Plate 94

U.S. National Park Service, for Plates 47, 81

U.S. Naval Academy Museum, Annapolis, for Plates 105, 107, 108

The Trustees of the Victoria and Albert Museum, London, for Plates 15, 20, 35, 44, 64, 68 (All Crown Copyright reserved)

Dr Hermann W. Williams, for Plate 106

The Trustees of the Wallace Collection, London, for Plates 13, 16, 41, 51, 55, 56, 57

Preface

Almost forty years ago Bashford Dean brought forth his detailed *Catalogue of European Daggers* (1929). For most of the time since, this work, together with Sir Guy Laking's chapter on daggers in his monumental *Record of European Armour and Arms Through Seven Centuries*, has remained the standard general references in English for students of these weapons. In the succeeding decades, however, there have appeared numerous specialized studies of individual dagger types and of the products of various geographical areas which have considerably increased our knowledge of the field and also extended its boundaries. Claude Blair did much to summarize this growing corpus of information in his *European and American Arms* (London, 1962), but despite the fact that he packed an amazing amount of information into a few pages, the format and scope of his work were such that he had to confine himself to brief comments and descriptions. More recently, Heribert Seitz has been offering a German summary in his *Blankwaffen,* the first volume of which appeared in 1962, while the second volume is expected shortly. In all these forty years, however, there has been no book-length survey devoted entirely to daggers and fighting knives.

The present book, therefore, has been conceived as an attempt to fill this gap in arms literature. It is an effort to bring the work of Dean and Laking up to date and to present in English a concise statement of the state of our knowledge of the subject. Most of it represents a synthesis of the work of others. Only the American section is based directly on primary research. Nevertheless, it is hoped that the summary of fugitive sources from many languages will meet a real need among collectors in both England and America who have long lacked a readily available reference in this field in their own language.

In the preparation of this volume I have had the generous co-operation of many individuals who have given unstintingly of their time and knowledge. In particular I would like to thank Mr Claude Blair of the Victoria and Albert Museum, the editor of this series, for his thoughtful review and his many suggestions for improving the original version, and also Mr A. V. B. Norman, Assistant to the Director of the Wallace Collection, who read the original manuscript and also vouchsafed corrections and suggestions for additional material.

Among the host of others who proffered assistance, I should especially like to mention Miss Winifred Needler of the Royal Ontario Museum: Mr Edgar Howell and Mr Craddock Goins, jun., of the Smithsonian Institution, Washington; Mr W. D. Thorburn of the Scottish United Services Museum, Edinburgh; Mr William Reid of the Tower of London; Dr Heribert Seitz of the Kungliga Armemuseum, Stockholm; Mr Eugen Heer of the Musée d'Art et d'Histoire, Geneva; Commander W. E. May and Mr Philip Annis of the National Maritime Museum, Greenwich; Mr Randolph Bullock and Dr Helmut Nickel of the Metropolitan Museum of Art, New York; Mr Norman Cook of the Guildhall Museum, London; and numerous private collectors, including Dr John K. Lattimer, Mr Leonard D. Pelton, Mr William C. Borland, Mr Bluford W. Muir, Mr Richard Lennington, and Mr Robert L. Klinger. I am deeply grateful to one and all.

H.L.P.
Arlington, Virginia, 1966

Chapter One

Origins of the Dagger and Fighting Knife

---◆---

Special knives for fighting are really a recent development. Man probably began to make stone knives some 500,000 years ago. But these knives were tools. They were designed for cutting and shaping wooden implements, scraping hides, preparing food, and for other utilitarian purposes. In an emergency one of these knives might have been used as a weapon, but it would have been very inefficient. For one thing, these implements were normally quite small and their primary function was to cut or scrape rather than to pierce. True, the so-called hand axe, the all-purpose tool that was widely used throughout much of the world in Paleolithic times, that is up till about 35000 B.C., often did have a pointed end. But it was not primarily a piercing instrument. A hand axe would have done more damage to an adversary than a bare fist, but almost any stone would have done just as well.

The true fighting knife did not appear until the Stone Age was almost over. Indeed, metal knives were already known before really good stone ones became common. There is even some speculation that the development of metal knives may have spurred the design of the stone weapons. Certainly, the very best of the stone daggers and fighting knives that appeared in Scandinavia about 1600 B.C. seem to have been made as almost direct copies of metal pieces.

By the time the stone knife had attained the weapon stage the techniques of stone working had reached their height. No more did the craftsman start out with a core pebble and gradually work it down to the desired size and shape with blows from a hammer stone or a wooden baton. Now, he struck off flakes of the approximate size he wanted and worked them down with controlled and precise pressure flaking. Then he often polished the completed knife to a beautiful finish.

Among the best of these Neolithic fighting knives were those made in such widely separated areas as Egypt and in Scandinavia. The Egyptian knives, usually made of a brownish or yellowish flint, boasted broad slightly curved blades perhaps 12 or 15 in long. The point was rounded and quite blunt, but the edges were sharp, and the piece was generally flat in cross-section. Sometimes the flaking scars were left over the entire surface of the blade. In other instances the centre section was polished smooth, and only the edges retained the flutes and serrations from the flaking process. The butt end or heel of the blade was inserted in a simple handle of wood, bone, horn, or ivory, and glued fast. There was no guard. A magnificent specimen of such a knife is now in the Louvre, Paris. The blade is a light yellow and finely shaped. The handle is of ivory elaborately carved with battle scenes. It dates from about 3500 B.C. In later years the hilt area of the stone blade was sometimes narrowed and given a grip-shape with a bird's-head pommel, so that a separate grip of organic material was unnecessary (Plate 1). Handsome as these Egyptian curved knives were, they were by no means ideal as weapons. They were brittle, and the long thin blades were especially susceptible to breakage. The shorter ones may have been useful in combat, but it is quite likely that the long knives were intended primarily for ceremonial purposes.

The Scandinavian daggers at first suffered from the same frailty as the Egyptian types. Stone, after all, is a brittle material that makes long slender shapes impractical. The Scandinavian dagger-makers, however, overcame this by shifting to thicker and broader blades, especially in the later forms. The Stone Age in northern Europe persisted later than it had in the south, and thus the peak of the Scandinavian stone knife and dagger development occurred well after the Mediterranean area had entered the Bronze Age. At that time knives and daggers became so popular and so important that archeologists have named the period from 1800-1500 B.C. the *Dolktid* or Dagger Period of Scandinavian prehistory.

The natural materials found in the north were magnificent, and the Stone Age craftsmen made the most of them. Flint was available in large pieces, and it ranged in colour from light yellowish tint through amber to a dark brown, almost black. Quartzite

I. Egyptian stone knife of Djer, a king of the first dynasty, *c.* 3009 B.C. The handle area is wrapped in gold foil. *Royal Ontario Museum, Toronto*

2. Early Scandinavian stone knife of the Dagger Period, *c.* 1800–1500 B.C. *Statens Historiska Museum, Stockholm*

3. Later Scandinavian stone knife with distinct handle and flaring butt, still of the Dagger Period. *Statens Historiska Museum, Stockholm*

4. Bronze dagger from Talyche or Luristan, *c.* 1400 B.C.–600 B.C. *Author's collection*

5. Bronze dagger from Luristan, a type that remained in use from about 1800 B.C.–600 B.C. *Author's collection* .

6. Bronze eared dagger from Luristan, *c.* 1000 B.C. *William C. Borland Collection*

7. Hallstatt dagger with iron blade and bronze hilt of the key form. The scabbard also is bronze. *Naturhistorisches Museum, Vienna*

8. Single-edged dagger from Hallstatt Period with gold-plated hilt and scabbard. *Naturhistorisches Museum, Vienna*

9. Bronze dagger from the Rhône district of France, dating near the end of the Early Bronze Age, perhaps 1450 B.C. *British Museum*

10. Dagger with antennae grip from the end of the Hallstatt Period. *Schweizerisches Landesmuseum, Zurich*

11, 12. Frankish scramasaxes of the sixth century. *Metropolitan Museum of Art, New York*

13. French rondel dagger with wooden grips and steel rondels, *c.* 1440–1450. *The Wallace Collection, London*

14. English rondel dagger with pierced grip, *c.* 1450. *Guildhall Museum, London*

15. Rondel dagger and scabbard of the type associated with Burgundy, late fifteenth century. *Victoria and Albert Museum, London*

16. Late rondel dagger and scabbard of the first half of the sixteenth century with tubular grip and blade of triangular section. *Wallace Collection, London*

17. Baselard of the common form with double-edged blade, fourteenth or very early fifteenth century. *Author's collection*

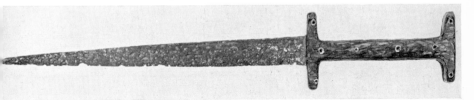

18. Baselard with single-edged blade, fourteenth century. *Author's Collection*

19. Baselard with carved boxwood hilt, probably Flemish, about 1400. *Metropolitan Museum of Art, New York*

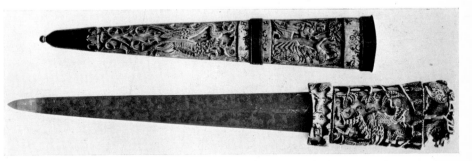

20. Elaborate baselard with carved ivory hilt and silver mounted ivory sheath, Italian, early fourteenth century. *Victoria and Albert Museum, London*

21. Swiss baselard with curved metal shod crosses, fourteenth to fifteenth century. *Schweizerisches Landesmuseum, Zurich*

22. (*left*) Quillon dagger with antennae pommel, excavated in London, mid fourteenth century. *Guildhall Museum, London*

23. (*centre*) Quillon dagger with crescent pommel, late fourteenth to early fifteenth century. *Schweizerisches Landesmuseum, Zurich.*

24. (*right*) Quillon dagger with ring pommel, late fourteenth century. *Schweizerisches Landesmuseum, Zurich*

25. Quillon dagger of the sword hilt form, English, late fourteenth century. *Guildhall Museum, London*

26. So-called Burgundian heraldic dagger with hollow wheel pommel, early fourteenth century. *Schweizerisches Landesmuseum, Zurich*

27. (*left*) So-called Burgundian dagger with hollow pommel and specifically heraldic inlay, early fourteenth century. *Schweizerisches Landesmuseum, Zurich*

28, 29. (*right*) Burgundian heraldic daggers with hollow star-shaped pommels, first half of the fourteenth century. *Musée d'Art et Histoire, Geneva*

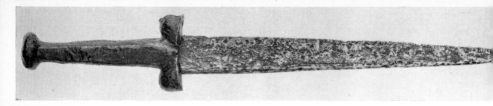

30. Ballock knife with phalliform hilt, fifteenth century. *Author's collection*

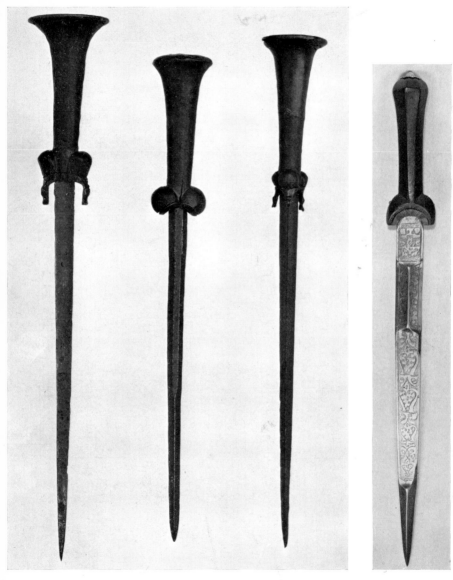

31, 32, 33. Ballock knives with inverted cone grips. Number 31 has arms projecting down the blade from the basal washer; number 33 has three basal eminences and arms. All are French or Flemish and date from the second half of the fifteenth century. *Metropolitan Museum of Art, New York*

34. *(right)* Late ballock dagger dated 1605 and made either in northern England or southern Scotland. This form is considered by many to be the direct ancestor of the Scottish dirk. *Victoria and Albert Museum, London*

could be obtained in black, green, red, and white. Probably no other area of the world offered a wider variety of excellent knife-making stone. The earliest of the fine daggers that the Scandinavians produced from this fine material were long, slender, diamond-shaped blades (Plate 2). Gradually one end of the diamond became more parallel-sided and rounded in cross-section to form a handle. Then the butt end began to flare slightly to offer a firmer grip. Eventually the handsome fully developed dagger appeared. It had a broad leaf-shaped blade, thick enough for reasonable strength. The narrowed grips were rounded or four-sided in section and thicker than the blade, and the butt or pommel flared widely. Down one side of the grips the flaking produced a narrow ridge that ran all the way from the pommel to the base of the blade. It served no useful purpose, but many students have viewed it as an attempt to copy in stone the seam of a leather-covered grip. Indeed, it is the widely held belief that these fine daggers are actually copies of bronze weapons that had already begun to move north through trade routes from southern Europe and the Mediterranean. These fully developed daggers had appeared by about 1600 B.C., and they continued to be made even after bronze weapons became relatively common in the centuries following 1500 B.C. (Plate 3).

Stone had offered ancient man a hard dense material that would take and hold a very sharp edge. It was a difficult material to work, however, and so the forms into which it could be shaped were limited. They were also limited by the brittle nature of stone when it was fashioned thin enough to be sharp. Knife and dagger blades broke easily, and once a stone knife was broken it was useless. It could not be repaired. A new material was needed before better, more practical fighting knives could be developed.

This new material was, of course, metal. It had both greater strength and greater plasticity than stone. When its use was mastered it offered a wider variety of shapes and sizes than had ever been possible before. It could be worked more easily, and it was repairable or at least reusable.

The first metal to be mastered was copper. Almost pure copper deposits are found in several parts of the world, including Mesopotamia, Egypt, India, and the Great Lakes region of North America. In each of these areas the people discovered the ores and began to use them in the manufacture of knives among other things. Archaeologists disagree on exact dates, but the general consensus is that copper knives and daggers were being made in Egypt, Mesopotamia, and other parts of the Near East by about 6500 B.C., at a slightly later date in India, and perhaps as early as 5500 B.C. in North America. In all instances, however, these nearly pure deposits of metal were small and soon became exhausted. Before that time was reached artisans in the Near East, Egypt, and India had learned to smelt copper from various ores. Their supply then became nearly unlimited. The American Indians, on the other hand, never learned to smelt copper, and so it remained a scarce and treasured commodity among them.

Pure copper is a durable, but relatively soft metal. It presented many problems to knife-makers. If a blade were to be made strong enough not to crumple under the force of a stabbing blow, it had to be made thick or wide. Increasing the thickness of blade increased its weight proportionately more than increasing its width, and weight was objectionable both because more metal was needed and because a heavier blade was harder to handle. Thus, the earliest copper daggers were usually short broad triangles, flat on both sides and seldom more than 6 ins. long. This stage was soon passed when it was found that the length of a blade could be increased by making the sides parallel for a short distance from the hilt, and this gave rise to the so-called ogival blade. Both the flat triangular and the flat ogival blades could be produced with the simplest forms of copper technology. They could be either cut and hammered into shape or cast in one-piece moulds. The edges could be considerably hardened and sharpened by hammering them when they were cold, and the resulting product was a crude but serviceable blade, a great improvement over stone.

Normally, all early copper daggers were hilted separately with wood, bone, ivory, or horn. Usually, the ancient designers solved the problem of joining hilt and blade by riveting the two together. The hilt was either slit or made in two pieces, and a portion of the heel of the blade was inserted in it. In many instances the heel of the blade was narrowed and extended farther up into the hilt in the form of a tang. Sometimes, however, blades are found with no signs of rivets, and it can only be assumed that they were glued in place in the manner of the earlier stone knives.

As time wore on it was found that dagger blades could be

stiffened by thickening them in the centre and by creating a strong mid-rib. This was possible only with a two-piece mould, but as soon as that advance in technology had been made daggers with such stiffening ribs began to appear, and they spread throughout the whole of Egypt and the Near East.

An even bigger step towards the production of better knives and daggers was the discovery of bronze. There are many theories about the method by which the discovery was made, but no matter how it came about, it offered a great improvement in materials for dagger and knife manufacture. Bronze is an alloy of copper mixed with a small amount of another metal. In the Bronze Age it was usually tin, and the best proportion was 90 per cent copper to 10 per cent tin. This ideal was seldom achieved, however, for the technology of the period was far from precise. Alloys with as little as 1 or 2 per cent of tin are encountered, and often daggers of almost pure copper were made at late dates well after the advantages of bronze were presumably understood. Bronze was a harder metal than copper and it flowed better in casting. It thus opened the door to the making of more elaborate designs and stronger weapons. Blades could be made thinner and longer without the danger of crumpling in use. Metal hilts could be produced, and sometimes they were cast in one piece with the blade, thus avoiding the potentially weak joint between the two elements.

As early as 2500 B.C. the Sumerians at Ur in Mesopotamia were making fine bronze daggers with ribbed blades and strong tangs. Within the next few centuries they developed separate bronze guards and spectacular crescentic pommels. Bronze Age centres in the Near East such as Talyche and Luristan were manufacturing one-piece daggers in distinctive designs with recesses in the hilts to receive plaques of wood or bone—the first scales to appear in knife manufacture (Plates 4 & 5). A little later the Near East brought forth a design with a solid bronze grip and flaring eared pommels that was to reappear in all its essentials except materials in medieval Europe (Plate 6). Egypt, too, produced one-piece daggers with beautifully ribbed blades and bigger, slightly more crescentic pommels than those of Luristan and Talyche.

The Bronze Age came to Europe through the trade routes to the Mediterranean. The principal European trade material at the time seems to have been amber, and so bronze culture first followed the route up the Danube and down the Elbe to the source for this substance in northern Europe. The date cannot be pinpointed, but people in this area were well aquainted with bronze implements before 1600 B.C. Other parts of Europe obtained bronze articles and began to produce the metal themselves at a later date. Within a few years specialized and readily identifiable European dagger forms began to appear. One of the earliest consisted of a short flat triangular blade with a round heel (Plate 9). Very often it was adorned with a series of grooves parallel to the edges of the blade which joined each other in the centre line. The hilt came down over the heel of the blade in a semi-circular fashion and riveted fast. The grips were a simple cylinder, and the pommel a flat cap. In the beginning these hilts were normally made of organic materials such as wood, horn, or bone. According to V. Gordon Childe in his standard work, *The Bronze Age,* one or two specimens have survived from England and Brittany complete with such wooden hilts all studded with tiny gold nails. Another, in the British Museum, from Wiltshire, has thirty-two bronze rivets through the wood of the hilt. Before the end of the Early Bronze Age (about 1500-1450 B.C. on the Danube trade route) these hilts were being cast in bronze in northern Italy, the Rhône Valley, and central Europe. From these areas they spread to other parts of Europe by way of subsidiary trade routes. In Germany daggers of the same pattern were cast with the hilt and blade in one piece. Decoration on these all-bronze daggers consisted of incised lines in geometric patterns. Often, there were two series of these lines encircling the grips, perhaps in imitation of the wrappings that might have held a two-piece hilt together.

During the Middle Bronze Age a few modifications of these types began to appear. In the Rhône Valley an ogival blade evolved out of the earlier form. It retained the same flat section, rounded heel, and the characteristic incised line decoration. In central Europe the new form was quite different. Most noticeable was its central mid-rib, though this was sometimes quite broad and ill defined. Also the heel became trapeze-shaped. In the earlier specimens this heel was quite broad and carried six rivets for the attachment of the hilt. In later years the heel narrowed until frequently only two rivets remained. Another characteristic of the central European dagger was its plainness. Normally there was no decoration of any kind. Far to the north a third form developed with an ogival blade bearing a central mid-rib. Unlike the central European form, it was frequently decorated, especially the hilt, which was sometimes cast to resemble thong wrappings and sometimes inlaid or overlaid with gold. All three of these later dagger forms retained the cylindrical grips and the flat plate pommel.

Meanwhile another metal had been added to the workshop of the knife- and dagger-makers of the Near East; this was iron. Like copper, iron was occasionally found in a pure state in the form of meteors, and the first iron to be worked by man undoubtedly came from such sources. Indeed, the ancient Sumerian word for iron means 'heaven-metal', and the Egyptians called it 'black copper from the skies'. As early as 3000 B.C. men were fashioning such natural iron into ornaments in Egypt and several areas of the Near East. Then it was found that heating and hammering some of the red and yellow earths that had been used for paints would also produce iron, and the sources for the new metal increased immeasurably.

This early iron was wrought iron. It was soft and would not take as sharp an edge as hardened copper or bronze. It was completely unsuitable for making knives or cutting tools. Hardening iron was a more complicated process than hardening copper and its alloys. What is more, it was done in almost the reverse manner. Instead of cold hammering, iron had to be heated in a charcoal fire and then hammered, reheated and hammered again through a long process. As this was done, the iron picked up carbon from the charcoal fire and really became a form of steel. Steel actually is only iron with from 1 to 5 per cent of carbon added. Final hardening came by heating the steel and plunging it into water or some other liquid to cool it quickly in a process known as tempering. Hardening iron by picking up carbon from a charcoal fire is known as steeling. It was a haphazard process at best and its results were far from uniform, but it did produce usable knives that were sharper and tougher than any made in the Bronze Age. What was more the supply of iron ore was far greater in quantity and wider in distribution than that of copper. And it was infinitely more widespread than tin. With the discovery of hardened iron or steel, knives and daggers could not only be made better, they could also be made more cheaply. Consequently they became much more common.

The first people known to have learned the technique of steeling iron were the smiths living in the Anatolian mountains, and they made the discovery about 1500 B.C. This area lay within the Hittite Empire, and its rulers jealously guarded the power that the new metal gave them. They refused to allow their own smiths to go abroad or to let foreigners learn the secret. Within a few centuries, however, seafaring peoples invaded the empire and learned, by force of arms, the technique of steeling iron, and spread it farther by their conquests. Among the invaders were the Philistines, who moved on to the coastal areas of Palestine near Canaan, where their fine steeled weapons gave them an advantage in battle over the Hebrews until the time of Saul and David at the turn of the first millennium B.C. The giant Goliath, in fact, is reported in the Bible to have carried an iron dagger or short sword in his battle with David as well as an iron-headed spear. The eventual defeat of the Philistines by the Hebrews brought the Iron Age to the Jews between 1025 and 975 B.C. By about 700 B.C. hardened iron daggers were being made in Greece and Egypt, and within another hundred years the Iron Age had spread as far as Britain and India. Well before the time of Christ all the major civilized areas of Europe and the Near East had entered the Iron Age.

In Europe iron was at first used to imitate the same forms of knives and daggers that had been manufactured in bronze and copper. Then, gradually, new designs began to appear. The rich finds from the Hallstatt Culture of central Europe, dating from the seventh to the fifth centuries B.C., present an excellent picture of the evolution from bronze forms to newer designs. For the first century or so the older bronze forms prevail. Then the new types begin to appear. Typical among them are handsome daggers with double-edged blades. The rusting process to which iron is susceptible makes it difficult to be absolutely sure of form, but some definitely tapered evenly from hilt to point, while some may have been convex or even slightly leaf-shaped in contour. Some were flat and some diamond-shaped in cross-section, with a slight median ridge. Single-edged blades are also encountered.

Hilts were often of bronze, sometimes overlaid with gold and occasionally set with pearls. One especially handsome form has been called the 'key grip', because it somewhat resembles a large house key (Plate 7). The grips are no longer simple cylinders, but often expand at the centre. The pommel shape, which is the outstanding characteristic of the key-grip daggers, is a flat oval in the same plane as the blade. It is often pierced to form an open-work design, very like the bow of a key. The lower part of the hilt overlaps the heel of the blade either in a straight line or with the ends turned forward along the blade at right-angles. Sometimes there is a slightly curved overlap reminiscent of the Bronze Age hilts. Looking less like a key, is another type of Hallstatt hilt in which the pommel forms two pierced discs or wheels (Plate 8). Typical also is the so-called antennae hilt (Plate 10). In this the pommel consists of two up-curving arms or horns. On the antennae daggers that appeared late in the Hallstatt Culture there is usually a guard curving in the opposite direction from the arms of the pommel. Sometimes a small ball like a stylized human head is added between the arms of the pommel, and the combination of the grips, the arms of the pommel and guard becomes quite anthropomorphic.

About 400 B.C. the Celtic La Tène Culture began to supersede the Hallstatt Culture. With this change, fewer and fewer double-edged daggers were made; single-edged knives predominated. Their blades resemble a butcher knife with the back straight and the edge curving up to meet it at the point. The tang was normally in line with the back, and it usually terminated at the pommel end either in a loop or a right-angle bend. Knives of this form were efficient all-purpose implements, useful either for general work and eating or for fighting. They were not handsome, however. They lacked the decorative features and the variety of forms of the Hallstatt daggers, and one must assume therefore that they quite possibly held a less important place in the culture of the people who employed them.

For the next millennium the fighting knife continued in its cultural nadir. The dagger was of little importance in the Roman civilization, and other weapons were preferred for combat by the northern migratory peoples of the period. Such knives as were made and used in the north seem to have continued to be single-edged La Tène forms. Then came the Viking Period of the ninth and tenth centuries, and the big knife emerged from its eclipse in the form of the famous scramasax (Plates 11 and 12). This was the all-purpose knife of the Northmen, the Germans, the Franks, and the Anglo-Saxons. The name *scramasax* actually is a modern adaptation of an ancient word of indeterminate meaning. A *sax* seems to have been a sword, possibly a single-edged sword. The prefix *scrama* might have meant 'wound maker', but even this is unclear. In any event, archeologists by convention have adopted the name *scramasax,* or sometimes *hand sax,* to refer to the great knives of these peoples.

In this context the scramasax was an imposing weapon as well as a general-purpose knife. Their blades varied in length from as little as 4 in to as large as 20 or more inches, when they became in reality short swords. All were single-edged and triangular in cross-section with a generally even taper from back to edge. Unlike the ancestral knives of the La Tène Culture the edge of the scramasax was usually straight. The back might also be straight, so that the blade formed an elongated triangle; but more often, it paralleled the edge for the greater distance, then curved to meet it in a convex arc or angled toward it in a straight line to form a slanted point. Occasionally, the edge curved up slightly to meet the back, but the greater curve was always on the back. A broad tang ran through the hilt and riveted above the pommel.

Very few hilts have survived, but those that have are made of wood or bone. They indicate that there was frequently a fully developed pommel, flat-sided but round or onion-shaped in profile. The grips also were often flat-sided. There was no guard, and the base of the grips joined the blade on a diagonal line, frequently with a band of decoration.

Scabbards, too, are scarce, but those that survive are made of both leather and wood, and they conform fairly closely to the shape of the blade. The leather types are fastened along both edges with a series of large and small rivets of copper or bronze. In a few instances iron rivets seem to have been used also, but they have not survived the ravages of time. Metal mounts are rare, but at least one scabbard, now in the Metropolitan Museum of Art, bears a rudimentary reinforcement at the throat made of bronze. Wooden scabbards seem to have been made generally of two pieces, bound with bronze bands. Some wooden scabbards have suspension rings, but on others there is no provision for attachments of any kind. These latter knives must have been worn thrust through the belt, held in place only by friction.

The scramasax was a sturdy knife. The blades were comparatively broad, suitable for dealing a heavy blow in fighting. The design permitted either a cut or a thrust, though the cutting action seems to have been favoured. Examples are often decorated with inlaid runic alphabets, statements of ownership and manufacture.

Because of its effective design and general utility, the period of use of the scramasax was a long one. It seems to have appeared towards the close of the Migration Period, perhaps in the eighth century A.D., and its great era of popularity continued for about three or four centuries. Even after that it did not fall entirely from use, but continued to be carried and used by working-class people. In England, at least, knives of the scramasax form were still being made in the fifteenth century, when the Middle Ages were drawing to a close. A number of these late types have been found in London and are now in the London Museum.

With its extended period of use, the scramasax forms the transition from the simple late Iron Age knife forms of the La Tène Culture to the sophisticated flowering of the dagger and fighting knife in the Middle Ages. Few other knife forms have remained in use so long or been popular in so wide a geographical area.

Chapter Two

Medieval Daggers

The Middle Ages witnessed the real flowering of the fighting knife and dagger. New forms appeared, and variations multiplied in a manner, and on a scale, never before achieved. The demand was great. Almost everyone carried a knife or a dagger in his belt. Knights and men-at-arms used them as an adjunct to the sword when armed for war. Civilians wore them for self-protection, for general utility and also for eating. Labourers and peasants commonly carried daggers, and even women occasionally wore sheath knives, though theirs were smaller and definitely eating and utility knives rather than weapons. The dagger had assumed a cultural position it had never enjoyed before.

During the Middle Ages little imagination seems to have been displayed in the manner in which the fighting knife was used. True, warriors did occasionally throw their daggers into the faces of the enemy before attacking with their swords, but in general the knife was a simple stabbing weapon.[1] In a fight, one combatant usually tried to seize his opponent's knife arm with his left hand and hold it while he delivered his own blow. Strength rather than skill normally prevailed. Although a few contemporary portrayals of the dagger in use show it held with the blade above the hand in the modern fighting knife-fighting manner, the overwhelming evidence indicates that it was usually held with the blade below the hand. Such a grip limited the wielder to an efficient downward stroke and an awkward horizontal stroke. All of the flexibility and manoeuvrability prized by later generations of knife-fighters were denied the man who held his dagger in such a position. More than anything, it emphasized strength rather than speed. The one advantage of the

[1] Bashford Dean cites an instance in which the English threw their daggers at the French in 1386.

downward stabbing stroke was that it could be delivered with more power than any forehand thrust, and this may have been overridingly important in a day when an opponent might well have been wearing a shirt of mail or some form of padded armour.

The method of wearing the dagger also emphasized the popularity of the stabbing technique. Normally, the dagger was worn vertically in the front, vertically or at an angle on the right side, or almost horizontally across the back with the hilt to the right. In this last position the weapon could easily be drawn with the blade either above or below the hand. In the other two locations it could be drawn most conveniently with the blade below the hand in the stabbing grip. Sometimes the dagger was worn by itself; sometimes in conjunction with the pouch.

When it came to dagger design, however, there was imagination in plenty. The scramasax was, of course, the first of the important medieval fighting knives. In design and use, though, it related more closely to the earlier weapons of the late Iron Age than to the sophisticated daggers of the later Middle Ages, and so it has been treated in the previous chapter. The new age of the dagger began late in the thirteenth century, well after the scramasax had lost most of its popularity, and it introduced a whole sequence of weapons that was to continue through the Renaissance and into modern times, with one form developing directly from its predecessor. Generally speaking, seven major families of dagger appeared in western Europe between the late thirteenth century and 1500. There were also subsidiary forms and a number of variants. Because of this, it has become the custom to study medieval daggers first by type and only secondarily by chronology.

Rondel Daggers

In such an approach, one of the first families of daggers to distinguish might be the rondel (or roundel) daggers. This is a modern term used to designate a form of dagger characterized by a disc-shaped guard and frequently by a pommel of the same form, set at right-angles to the line of the hilt (Plate 13). Despite its lack of historical background it is an obvious descriptive term and has been widely accepted throughout the world, even in languages other than English. The French call it a *dague à rouelles* and the Germans a *Scheibendolch,* both referring to the same features.

There is some disagreement among historians about the date

of the rondel dagger's first appearance. Some place it is as early as 1300 or even slightly before. All agree, however, that the type was already in general use between 1325 amd 1350. It increased in popularity during the remainder of the fourteenth century and continued to be widely popular until about 1550. Its area of use extended from Scandinavia in the north to Spain in the south, from the British Isles on the west to Poland on the east, thus taking in almost all of western and central Europe. In all this area it was mainly a weapon of the knightly classes. Some few simple, slightly crude rondel daggers have survived, but the bulk of them are well-made specimens, usually with some form of decoration.

In the earliest forms of the rondel dagger only the guard was apt to be discoidal. Frequently it was deep, almost pillbox-shaped. Sometimes it was contructed from a piece of hard wood sheathed with iron. In at least a few instances it seems to have been hollowed out on the blade side so that it would fit down over the scabbard in locket fashion. This belief is based upon a few monumental brasses, such as that of Sir Edward Cerne, Draycott Cerne Church, Wiltshire, and other contemporary representations, and it is possible that the artist's intentions have been misread. No actual dagger with such a locket guard is known to survive. The pommels of these early rondel daggers assumed many forms. Some were disc- or wheel-shaped like the pommels of contemporary swords, and they stood on edge in the same fashion as sword pommels. Others were spherical, conical, or onion-shaped. In a few instances, contemporary illustrations seem to indicate that the grips simply terminated in a slightly bulbous shape without a true pommel, as seen on the brass of Sir Reginald de Cobham, Lingfield Church, Surrey, while in others the grips flared widely at the pommel end and were capped with a thin metal plate, achieving almost a rondel pommel, as in the painting of c. 1420 which was catalogued as No. 420 in the Bruges Exhibition of 1902. Yet true rondel pommels, similar to the guards, also appeared, and by about 1400 they had become almost universal; though one occasionally finds a pommel of another form appearing, as one finds 'foreign' forms appearing in all periods of the dagger's history. The grips of these fourteenth-century examples normally seem to have been made in one piece and drilled to allow the narrow tang of the blade to pass through and to be riveted at the pommel. The sides of the grips were usually straight or only slightly expanded in the centre, and the grips themselves might be round or faceted or even spirally grooved. Most blades were relatively short, double-edged and of flattened diamond shape in section. Generally they tapered evenly from hilt to point.

During the fifteenth century many changes took place. As noted above, the rondel pommel became almost universal, matching the guard. Sometimes the pommels became so large, especially in central Europe after 1450, that it is almost impossible to hold the weapon in anything but a stabbing grip, with the wide pommel above the thumb, further evidence of the popularity of the stabbing blow as the primary knife attack. Both pommels and guards were usually thinner than they had been. Sometimes they were made of a single solid plate of metal. Often they were composed of two convex plates fastened together around the edges. The composite construction of wood or bone and metal also continued and, about 1450, some pommels and guards were multi-layered with alternate discs of iron, bone, brass, wood, or horn. These multiple layers were designed for their decorative effect, and so the edges were left exposed to show the banding in different colours. Simpler composite discs, however, frequently had the top and bottom metal plates flanged so that they completely covered the inner core. The majority of the rondels were circular in outline, but a few were octagonal or hexagonal and a very few were fluted or irregularly contoured.

The grips of the rondel dagger also varied in both design and construction. The one-piece, generally cylindrical form, continued in use and spiral carving remained popular, but new forms began to appear. Grips composed of two plaques or scales, fitted on either side of a broad tang, came into use. Sometimes these scales were rounded, sometimes faceted. Frequently, they were attached with as many as three or four large rivets, the heads of which were often decorated. In a few instances these were ring rivets with little holes passing right through the grips. About 1450 a grip design appeared with a large swelling in the centre, pierced with a hole that passed directly through both grips and tang. Possibly this was for the attachment of a thong, but it seems an awkward location for such a feature. Surely a thong attached to the wrist and grasped by the hand as it fastened to the weapon must have interfered with the wielder's freedom of movement in striking a blow. Grips with a pronounced swelling in the centre (including, in some cases, a distinct ring) are known from both England and France, but the pierced grips have only been found on English examples (Plate 14). A final shape that became increasingly popular as the fifteenth century wore on found the grips tapering, often in a concave line, from pommel to guard.

The blades found on rondel daggers increased in length and variety. The evenly tapering double-edged blades continued in use, but single-edged blades became more common. These latter blades were sometimes triangular in section, sometimes slightly hollow ground. At times they reached the length of 15 or 16 in. Both double- and single-edged types occasionally had reinforced quadrangular points designed for piercing mail (Plate 15). A very few rondel daggers possessed narrow, but stout, quadrangular blades designed solely for piercing and foreshadowing the stilettos of the future.

Because of their widespread use and their general similarities, it is very difficult to assign most rondel daggers to a specific area of origin. There is one type which developed late in the fifteenth century, however, that can be traced to a single geographic area. It is an especially handsome form of the weapon, characterized by a rondel pommel that is convex on top, assuming a domed or mushroom shape. Sometimes the top of the pommel is faceted; more often it is fluted. The grips are normally straight-sided or slightly convex and are almost always carved. Sometimes this carving takes the form of flutes or deep checkering; sometimes it approximates the traditional Burgundian cross raguley or knotted cross. The usual materials for the hilts are wood or horn, often with brass fittings for decoration. A few are known of other materials, including rock crystal and silver. Since daggers of this readily recognizable form are illustrated in the famous Burgundian tapestries of the late fifteenth century and since some of them bear grips that seem to resemble the Burgundian cross raguley, students and collectors have classified them as made in, or for, Burgundy. They could just as well have been made and used in Switzerland and near by areas of Germany, however, and probably they were. But still, it provides a closer area of provenance than most daggers of the rondel form.

During the first half of the sixteenth century the evolution of the rondel dagger led generally towards decadence. Some of the earlier forms, including the Burgundian design, continued, but blades tended to become longer and thinner. Pommels increased in size, while guards shrank (Plate 16). In some south German forms the guards even lost their rondel form and broke into lobes that bent down over the blade, perhaps a transition to the Landsknecht dagger of that century. In keeping with the general Renaissance tastes of this era, surface enrichment increased, and the most highly decorated of the rondel daggers are these latest examples of the form. The strength and character of the early types, however, are almost entirely gone.

Throughout the period of the rondel dagger's evolution its scabbard kept pace with the changes in design. In the fourteenth century the scabbards were simple sheaths that fitted the blade closely and terminated at the forward edge of the guard. No examples of the sheaths of this early type have survived, but monumental brasses seem to indicate that they had metal throats and chapes and that the leather body was often tooled with various designs, while the metal mounts also were decorated. In the fifteenth century metal mounts became rare. The entire scabbard was made of leather, and the throat was expanded so that it fit up over the rondel of the guard. A few examples of such fifteenth century scabbards are still preserved in museum collections and indicate that they were indeed often decorated with tooling as the earlier type seems to have been. Scabbards of the late fifteenth and early sixteenth centuries illustrate the influence of the Renaissance in their surface enrichment. Since the blades of the daggers of the period were frequently long and slender, the scabbards are also long, and their length is usually broken up into zones of decoration in embossed and sculptured leather. Frequently, there is a long metal chape and often there is a metal throat and sometimes even bands about the body of the sheath, all of them decorated with relief designs. The enlarged mouth that received the rondel in the middle types is completely missing on these later examples. Except for the character of their decoration and their length, they more closely resemble the scabbards of the fourteenth century.

Baselards

The second of the major families of dagger types to be considered here was perhaps the most widely used of all. Arms students today call this type of dagger a baselard, and there is every indication that they are using the proper historical term. The word appears with great frequency in documents of the fourteenth and fifteenth centuries where daggers are discussed. This is especially true of English texts, but the name appears in other languages as well. From its use, it is quite evident that it was a specific name, not a generic term. Also, it obviously applied to a very popular dagger worn throughout Europe. By a process of elimination and comparison, historians deduced that it must have indicated a form of dagger of the period that they had also noticed appearing in great quantity in contemporary paintings, on brasses and on effigies, and which is also well represented by surviving specimens. A recent discovery in the Datini archives at Prato, in Italy by Claude Blair of the Victoria and Albert Museum seems at last to confirm the traditional thinking. This find, in a list of daggers purchased in 1375, indicates that the term baselard derived from the city of Basel in Switzerland and that the type originated there. Since the close affiliation between Switzerland and the form of dagger historians had come to call a baselard has long been recognized by all, the newly found document seems to settle the question of the baselard's identity once and for all. The term has been used correctly.

The baselard first appeared perhaps as early as the late thirteenth or early fourteenth centuries and, as noted above, probably originated in Switzerland. From there, it quickly spread throughout central and western Europe. The great bulk of documentary and iconographic references stem from the middle fourteenth century and later, for the dagger seems to have achieved its greatest popularity about that time. It continued in wide use until the late fifteenth century, when it evolved almost imperceptibly into the so-called Swiss dagger or Holbein dagger.

People from almost all walks of life carried baselards. In the fourteenth century it was a knightly weapon, frequently worn when fully armed for the field. This is especially true of Italian and south German knights, but there is evidence, notably the effigy of Sir Hugh Caeveley in Banbury Church, Cheshire, that the practice was not confined to that area. In addition to the warriors, civilians of many stations also carried the baselard to such an extent that the anonymous English writer of a satirical song of the period of Henry V, quoted by Laking, declared that:

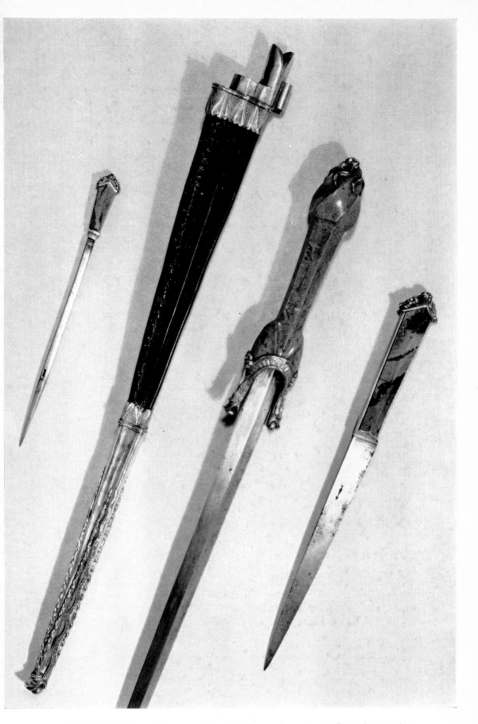

35. Ballock knife and accessories of Johann Amerbach-Ortenberg who died in 1513. The hilt is of agate with silver gilt mounts. The scabbard is of tooled leather, also with silver gilt mounts.
Historisches Museum, Basel

36. (*left*) Eared dagger of about 1500, probably Italian. The ears and guard are faced with ivory, the grip with horn. *Metropolitan Museum of Art, New York*

37. (*centre left*) Side view of the same dagger

38. (*centre right*) Eared dagger of the mid sixteenth century, probably Spanish. The hilt and blade are forged from one piece of steel. Note the widely flaring ears. *Metropolitan Museum of Art, New York*

39. (*right*) Eared dagger of degenerate form, probably Spanish *c.* 1550. Hilt and blade are forged from one piece of steel. *Metropolitan Museum of Art, New York*

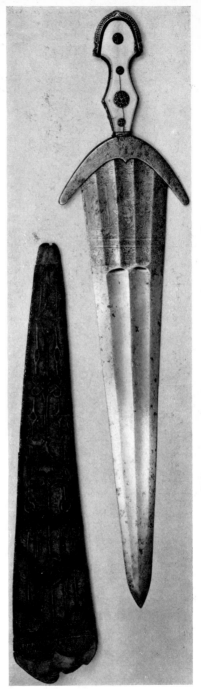

40. (*left*) Cinquedea with wheel pommel, and sword-like hilt, early
sixteenth century. *Metropolitan Museum of Art, New York*

41. (*right*) Cinquedea of the commoner form with arched pommel and
shaped tang, late fifteenth or early sixteenth century. The scabbard
of cuir bouilli originally had metal mounts which are now missing.
The Wallace Collection, London

42. Peasant knife or *Hauswehre*, with bolster and projection on the obverse side to protect the knuckles. Probably Swiss, sixteenth century. *Musée d'Art et d'Histoire, Geneva*

43. Peasant knife or *Hauswehre* with quillons, probably Swiss, fifteenth century. This specimen is somewhat unusual in that it has a pommel instead of a simple cap. *Bernisches Historisches Museum*

44. Swiss dagger with gilt scabbard portraying the death of Virginia and dated 1592. *Victoria and Albert Museum, London*

45. So-called Maximilian dagger, German, early sixteenth century. *Author's collection*

46. Dagger with vase-shaped pommel of the so-called "fish tail" pattern. Italian, *c.* 1525. *Metropolitan Museum of Art, New York*

47. Left-hand dagger and scabbard, late sixteenth century. The hilt and sheath mounts are damascened in gold; the wavy-edged blade is channelled and pierced. *U.S. National Park Service*

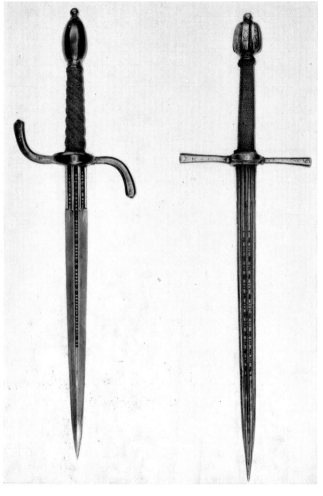

48. (*left*) Left-hand dagger with gilded hilt, Saxon, late sixteenth century. *Author's collection*

49. (*right*) Left-hand dagger, the hilt decorated with stamped ornament, late sixteenth century. *Author's collection*

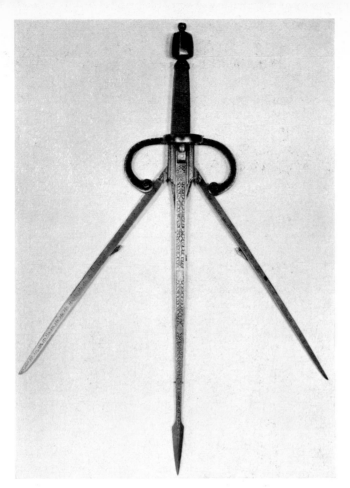

50. Left-hand dagger with triple blade, German, about 1600. In repose the two side blades fit tightly against the centre. Releasing a catch just below the side ring of the hilt causes them to fly apart under spring pressure until they are stopped by the ends of the quillons. The hilt is blued, the blade etched. *The Wallace Collection, London*

51. Sword breaker, probably Italian, about 1600. The ricasso is chiselled and gilt. *The Wallace Collection, London*

52. (*left*) Landsknecht dagger of the miniature katzbalger type, German, *c.* 1500. The horizontally S-curved quillons are bent so tightly they form almost a circle, terminating in ball finials. *Metropolitan Museum of Art, New York*

53. (*centre*) Landsknecht dagger of the more popular form, German, mid sixteenth century. *Metropolitan Museum of Art, New York*

54. (*right*) Saxon dagger of the Landsknecht form, German, *c.* 1580. The metal of the hilt is blued and enriched with engraved silver. The sheath mounts are silver and bear the marks of Dresden and of the goldsmith Wolf Paller who died in 1583. *Metropolitan Museum of Art, New York*

There is no man worth a leke,
Be he sturdy, be he meke,
But he bear a basilard.

In the fifteenth century, mounted knights generally ceased to carry the baselard and it became primarily the dagger of civilians and foot soldiers.

Baselards were worn generally in the same fashion as most other daggers, but there were some exceptions. Like the other types, they were often worn on the right side or suspended directly in front either from the sword belt or girdle or from a hanger attached to that belt. Seldom, if ever, were they carried at the back. Because baselards were sometimes long sword-like weapons, one also finds illustrations of them worn on the left side in the manner of a sword, and in one instance at least, the brass of John Corp (d. 1361) in Stoke Fleming Church, Devonshire, a baselard is suspended on the left side from a baldric slung over the right shoulder.

In form, the baselard can quickly be recognized by its hilt, which has a cross-piece at both the guard and pommel ends. This construction gives the hilt the appearance of a capital letter I or of an H laid on its side. In the usual construction, the tang of the blade follows the contour of the pommel cross-piece. Sometimes it also assumes the full shape and size of the cross at the guard; at others it expands in that area, but does not extend all the way to the ends. The grips are normally made in two pieces like scales and riveted through the tang. A large number of rivets are used, frequently three or four through the grips themselves and at least two on both the pommel and guard extensions. In many instances these are ring rivets which line tiny holes passing right through the hilt. The usual materials for the two side pieces of the hilt are organic—wood (often ivy or box root), horn, bone, or ivory (Plate 17). No metal hilts are known to the writer, although they may have been used on rare occasions.

Although they retained the basic form of a captial I, the exact shape of baselard hilts varied considerably. The grips themselves were usually straight-sided and quite slender, just the width of the blade tang. In some instances, however, the grips are broader and expand at both ends in a concave line, so that they blend into he upper and lower cross-pieces. But the greatest variation is to be found in the size and shape of these latter processes. Sometimes they are almost diminutive; sometimes so wide that each piece equals the length of the grips. In some instances both crosses may be of the same length, but often they differ, usually with the pommel the longer of the two. These crosses may be straight and parallel or they may slant away from the grips. Less commonly they may be curved either towards or away from the grips. In most instances, these processes are the same thickness as the corresponding structures on the tang, so that the metal may be seen as a band on both the top and bottom. Frequently, however, the crosses, especially at the guard, are at least a little longer than the tang processes and so the two side-pieces join together and conceal the metal at the ends.

The typical baselard blade tapers evenly from hilt to point. A few are single-edged, sometimes with a single narrow and shallow groove at the back. Some authorities consider the single-edged blade the earliest form, and most agree that it was confined primarily to the fourteenth century (Plate 18). Double-edged blades seem to have appeared very early also, however, and they are by far the more common among surviving examples (Plate 19). Usually they are a flattened diamond-shape in cross-section, and sometimes they bear two deep grooves in the centre that run from the hilt perhaps half or two-thirds the length of the blade. A few have a flat ricasso near the hilt before the edged portion of the blade begins. In size, the blades vary all the way from small dagger to sword proportions.

Surviving scabbards for baselards are rare in the extreme, and most information about their appearance must come from iconographic sources. These indicate that the body of the scabbard was usually of leather with metal mounts consisting of a throat, a middle band and a chape. Some paintings which show simply a black sheath of the same form as the blade it housed seem to indicate that scabbards of plain leather also were used, and there is one painting attributed to Giovanni dal Ponte in the Yale University Museum which suggests that the baselard was sometimes simply thrust through a narrow hanger and worn with the blade bare. At the other end of the scale are surviving scabbards in the Hermitage Museum, Leningrad, and the Victoria and Albert Museum, London, which are of the greatest luxury. They are made of carved ivory or bone, sometimes with metal tips (Plate 20).

Aside from the general run of baselards, there are two distinctive types which merit special mention. One of these comprises a group with elaboratively carved hilts of boxwood, bone, or ivory. In most cases, the ornamentation seems to be romanesque in inspiration, featuring dragons, animals, grotesque human figures, and intertwining traceries. On some specimens the upper and lower crosses remain, on some they are vestigial, and on still others they are gone completely. In this last group, the hilt is almost straight-sided, with no suggestion of any pommel or guard, yet most students still class them with the baselards. Both northern Italy and France have been suggested as the place of origin for daggers of this form, and they have usually been assigned to the fourteenth century. As with many forms of weapons that are both scarce and luxurious, these daggers have been especially attractive to forgers, primarily during the late nineteenth and very early twentieth centuries.

The second distinctive form of baselard comprises those types with curved metal-shod crosses (Plate 21). In almost all instances these crosses curve towards each other, but very occasionally one is encountered with the lower cross bending towards the blade. Unlike the usual baselard, the tang on these specimens is narrow, and the grips are usually one-piece instead of two. The grips, almost always of wood, are straight-sided and usually taper slightly from pommel to guard. The metal plates which cover the upper edge of the pommel-cross and the lower edge of the guard are normally quite thin in the early specimens. Each is usually held in place by two little nails as well as by the pressure from the tang rivet. Later types boast heavier metal plates which are sometimes thickened at the ends to form the full width of the crosses. One of these daggers has been found in Brooks Wharf, London, and is now in the Guildhall Museum. This is a rare find, however. The form is generally very closely associated with Switzerland, where there are both iconographic representations and surviving specimens in quantity. It is, in all major respects, the so-called Swiss dagger of the sixteenth century.

Quillon Daggers

In reality, the lower cross of the baselard was a form of quillon. Yet because of its peculiar hilt structure and its great popularity, the baselard has always been ranked separately and not as a part of the family of so-called quillon daggers. This large and varied classification has been named by arms historians on the basis of the dagger guards which often resemble the quillons (cross-bars) of contemporary swords. In fact, many quillon daggers are really diminutive copies of the sword in all respects. This is especially true in those instances when sword and dagger were made *en suite* as a pair of weapons. In such cases, pommels, grips, guards, and decoration often match and sometimes blade shapes are similar. There are other quillon daggers, however, which resemble the sword only in the fact that they have a distinct cross-guard. Among these are such sub-groups as the antennae-pommel and ring-pommel daggers and those with simply a butt-cap instead of a true pommel.

Among the first of the quillon daggers to appear were the antennae-pommel types which possibly developed in the thirteenth century (Plate 22). In appearance these weapons are strikingly similar to the antennae types of the Hallstatt period. Both pommel and quillons are separate pieces that fit over the tang and both curve away from the grips. They either terminate in small flat-sided lobes or else the ends are rolled back on themselves to form tiny loops on the sides away from the grips. The tang of the blade is narrow, and so the grips must obviously have been made in one piece, drilled for the tang to pass through. No specimen is known to retain its original grips, however, and the writer knows of no contemporary pictorial data to indicate their form or decoration. Blades are almost always double-edged and diamond-shaped in cross-section. They taper evenly in a straight or slightly convex line from hilt to point. Antennae daggers were never widely popular. As noted above, no iconographic source is known to the author. Only a few specimens have survived—all excavated—but they have been found in locations ranging from England to Switzerland, so that a wide area of use is indicated. The consensus of opinion among students is that this early form of the antennae dagger disappeared after about 1350.

Two offshoots of the early antennae form, however, lasted perhaps another fifty years. These daggers boasted pommels in the form of crescents or rings. In the crescent daggers, the pommel is made very much as it was on the antennae types, but there are distinct differences. The bar is usually thicker, and the curve is more sudden, sometimes almost completing a circle

(Plate 23). Also the terminal lobes or roll-overs are missing, and the ends of the bar are commonly slightly pointed. The guard is usually straight or slightly curved towards the blade, again without the terminal lobes or roll-overs. Another distinct difference is that the tang is broad and pierced for rivets, so that the grips must have been made in two pieces. The blade usually tapers evenly from hilt to point, but it is almost always single-edged, and there is often a narrow groove at the back which runs about two-thirds of its length.

The ring daggers are closely allied to this group. Some of the crescent pommels are, in fact, almost rings (Plate 24). In the fully developed ring dagger, however, the ring is fashioned as a part of the tang and not as a separate piece, as it seems always to have been in the antennae and crescent types. Again, the tang is broad and usually pierced for rivets to hold the two-piece grips. The guard is apt to be short and curved slightly towards the blade. Some of the surviving specimens retain small nails passing up through the guard. Obviously these nails must have gone into the grips, and since they are out beyond the width of the broad tang it would seem to indicate that the grips must have expanded at the base or perhaps flared out over the guard in the fashion of the later Swiss baselards. Unlike the crescent daggers, surviving specimens suggest that the blades of those with ring pommels were usually double-edged and diamond-shaped in cross-section.

Ring daggers of this type seem to have been popular only in central Europe and to have been confined largely to the fifteenth century. There were, however, other daggers with ring pommels. One form with a spool-shaped guard is known from England, where there are specimens in both the Guildhall and British Museums, and there are other examples of the use of the ring pommel with different classes of dagger. It was, after all, a functional feature that could be used for securing the weapon to the person, and so the quillon family had no monopoly of it.

Quillon daggers that closely resembled contemporary swords probably appeared about 1250 or shortly before. They are shown in the *Maciejowski Bible* of about that date, and they are found on effigies dating from early in the fourteenth century. The earliest recorded representations show a fully developed form. These daggers have pommels that range through all the versions found on swords of the period (Plate 25). There are disc pommels, wheel pommels, octagonal pommels, spherical pommels, and still other shapes. Grips might be either one- or two-piece, and English effigies at least indicate that they were frequently wrapped with wire or leather. The quillons sometimes closely resemble those found on swords of the period, but often they are shorter and commonly bend forward sharply or curl at the ends. The blades as a rule are quite short, and they may be either double-edged and diamond-shaped in cross-section or single-edged, triangular in section and often have a single groove at the back. Sometimes single-edged specimens dating from after 1450 or thereabouts have slightly hollow ground blades. Both types of blade normally taper evenly from hilt to point, but sometimes on the single-edged types the edge tapers gradually for most of its length and then turns sharply towards the point.

Scabbards are rare for early quillon daggers of the sword-hilt type. Effigies, brasses, and paintings, however, indicate that they were usually made of leather with metal throat and chape. Sometimes the leather appears to have been tooled, and the metal mounts are frequently decorated with arches, geometric designs, and occasionally with highly stylized foliage. The borders of both the throat and chape were frequently cut in a decorative manner, often with a series of small points, but they were also sometimes absolutely straight. In some instances there were slight wings on the chape.

Quillon daggers of this type seem to have been primarily knightly weapons. As such, they were usually worn on the right side, dependent from the sword belt. From the way they hang in the effigies and brasses it would seem that there was often a staple or a loop on the back of the throat so that they could be attached to the belt by a cord or thong.

Among the quillon daggers with sword hilts there is one special group that collectors and students have long called Burgundian or heraldic daggers (Plate 26). Some of them certainly were associated with Burgundy, but they were also popular in Switzerland and near-by areas of Germany. There are two or three distinct forms of these daggers, but all have certain similarities and all spring from the same area. One of their common characteristics is that they are often decorated with heraldic designs, and it is this factor which has given them their second designation. A second characteristic is that they have hollow pommels.

Specimens of the first sub-group of so-called Burgundian or heraldic daggers have wheel pommels with capstan rivets. The flat face of one or both sides of the pommel is usually inlaid with a disc of brass or copper over tin. These discs are usually engraved with foliate or geometric decorations that are not obviously heraldic. At the base of these pommels is a four-sided throat that passes down over the grips and is usually decorated in the same manner as the pommel disc. The guard springs from another throat or ferrule similar to that on the pommel. The quillons are short and curve slightly forward over the blade. They end in sharply bent terminals. They, too, often bear punched or engraved decorations. The wooden grips, which may be seen only for a short space between the two ferrules are also four-sided. The blades are almost always single-edged with the back and edge almost parallel to each other till they reach the point where the edge turns up sharply to meet the back.

The sub-group described above is not specifically heraldic. It is classified with the main type because of its hollow pommels and its area of origin. A second sub-group almost always bears definite heraldic designs on its pommels. These pommels may be disc, shield-shaped, polygonal, or even bulbously fig-shaped with six uneven sides, but always they are hollow, and on one face there is inlaid a shield with a lily, a lion or some other heraldic motif (Plate 27). They lack the collars or ferrules of the previous type and the quillons are simple bars that curve forward towards the blade in an arc. Sometimes they are decorated with straight file lines. The grips are usually lacking from surviving pieces, but in most instances they seem to have been made in two parts, held by three rivets which passed through the tang. In some instances, however, the grips appear to have been of one piece and drilled for a narrower tang. The blades of this sub-group are normally quite short and single-edged. Edge and back may taper evenly or the edge may curve up sharply near the point. Usually there is a narrow groove at the back.

The third sub-class of Burgundian daggers comprises a group with pommels shaped like a seven-pointed star (Plates 28 and 29). Both pommel and the four-sided grips are normally hollow and built up of several separate pieces of iron. The face of the pommel is usually inlaid with a brass disc that features an equestrian figure inside a border bearing an inscription. Both the figure and the inscription vary from one specimen to another. At least one specimen in the Charles Buttin collection was originally inlaid with gold instead of brass. The quillons are solid instead of being hollow like the pommel and grips, and they curve forward slightly towards the blade. Both guard and grips are frequently inlaid with more precious metals in various stylized designs. The blades may be single- or double-edged. Of all the daggers in this category, this is the form that is most closely and obviously associated with Burgundy. Almost all the surviving specimens have been found in the province or within a few miles of its borders.

All of the Burgundian or heraldic daggers are considered to be early types by arms historians. There was a time when many were thought to date from the thirteenth or even the twelfth centuries Now, however, the general consensus of opinion is that they belong to the period 1300-50.

Finally, there is one class of quillon daggers that is not considered sword-hilted. Daggers of this type either have a simple butt-cap or perhaps no cap at all on the end of the grips. These grips usually expand at least slightly towards the butt, and they may be treated in many ways—reeded, or carved with spiral grooves, little bosses, or facets. The quillons are usually short and thick and the blades may be either single- or double-edged. Daggers of this form seem to have become popular during the second half of the fourteenth century and to have gained in popularity during the next hundred years, though they were always a minor type. Most of the recorded specimens are from England, though at least one specimen of unknown provenance, in the Metropolitan Museum of Art, has been attributed to Burgundy, probably because the grips somewhat resemble the Burgundian cross raguley and are thus similar to the grips sometimes found on late Burgundian rondel daggers. It is probable that the type was really widespread, but being a simple form and seldom evincing fine workmanship, it has not attracted the attention of students.

So much for the quillon daggers of the Middle Ages. Most of the types described above fell from popularity and disappeared before 1500. They were succeeded by new forms, for the quillon dagger remained a principal family of weapons throughout the Renaissance and into modern times.

Ballock Knives (Kidney Daggers)

A fourth of the great families of medieval daggers was characterized by two rounded prominences in place of a guard (Plate 30). At the time, English writers called such a weapon a ballock knife and French writers a *dague à couillettes*. More prudish Victorian writers called it a kidney dagger. Since the Victorians were the first of the modern arms historians, their term has stuck until very recent years, when there has been a serious effort to return to accurate contemporary English usage in describing arms and armour. At one time there was an effort to reinforce the sexual derivation of the hilts of these daggers by stating that they were customarily worn directly at the front of the girdle. Actually, this was true primarily of the fourteenth century, and it was by no means universal then. Iconographic sources indicate that they were just as often worn at the right side. This became the common position in the fifteenth century, and they were often carried in a horizontal position, even slipping around to the back on occasion. There is no need for such external evidence, however. For one thing the name itself is quite indicative, and for another some of the surviving hilts are remarkably phalliform in their contours.

The ballock knife apparently first appeared about 1300. One of the earliest illustrations of it occurs in the Bohemian *Bilderbibel* of 1300-50 in the National Library, Vienna. It also appears on Continental effigies in a well-developed form before 1350, and becomes increasingly common both on the Continent and in the British Isles during the latter half of the fourteenth century and most of the fifteenth century. Excellent representations of it occur on the brasses of Sir William de Aldeburgh in Aldborough Church, Yorkshire (1360), and Robert Parys in Hildersham Church, Cambridgeshire (1379). The ballock knife continued in use on the Continent well into the sixteenth century, perhaps even into the second half, for it is commonly shown in Flemish paintings of the 1550s and 1560s. In England it persisted into the seventeenth century, and in Scotland it eventually evolved into the Scottish dirk. Early effigies and brasses indicate that the ballock knife was then a knightly weapon, and later elaborate surviving specimens such as that of Johann Amerbach-Ortenberg in the Historisches Museum, Basel, suggest that it was worn by the wealthy merchant class and nobility (Plate 35). It was also a weapon of the merchant and artisan class, however, and possibly also of the peasantry, for some extant examples are remarkably crude and simple.

In its simplest form, the ballock knife had a plain wooden hilt without any metal pieces whatsoever. The basal eminences were ample and well rounded, and the butt end terminated in a bulbous knob. The grips might taper either towards the pommel or the guard end. This hilt was made in one piece, frequently, in England at least, of boxwood. Boxwood was often called dudgeon at the time and this gave rise to another ancient name that was probably applied specifically to this weapon—dudgeon dagger. Other materials included ivy root, horn, ivory, bone, and on later specimens metal and even agate. Several historians have suggested that these one-piece hilts without metal plates of any sort were the earliest form of the quillon dagger. They may well have been, but they continued in use as the cheapest and simplest form well into the fifteenth century. Better-quality specimens, certainly by the early years of the fifteenth century, boasted shaped metal washers between the basal eminence and the blade and perhaps another washer on the pommel beneath the rivet of the tang.

At least by the opening years of the fifteenth century another hilt form of the ballock knife had appeared. The basal eminences remained the same, but the grips flared upwards almost in the form of an inverted cone, ending in a flat butt which was usually covered by a metal plate (Plates 31, 32 and 33). In the better examples this plate was brass engraved with geometric designs. This hilt form never supplanted the one with the bulbous butt. The two types continued in use contemporaneously as long as the ballock knife was manufactured. They were joined late in the fifteenth century by another form in which the grips were almost straight-sided with a flat or slightly rounded butt. These later grips might be smooth, faceted or carved in spirals or bosses. Sometimes they were capped. In other instances there was simply a small washer beneath the tang-rivet.

During the second half of the fifteenth century other developments took place at the guard end of the hilt. Most importantly the metal washer between hilt and blade that had appeared early in the century became thicker and developed arms which protruded down along the blade like sharply drooping quillons. In some daggers, notably those made in northern France, Flanders, or northern Germany, the basal lobes themselves were made of metal and protruded like short quillons. And finally, in this period also, a very few specimens are known to have been made with three lobes instead of the usual two. Some of these metal-lobed ballock knives, found in northern Germany also have metal discoidal pommels, a feature that seems to have been confined to this region.

Blade types for the ballock knife varied. In the beginning the commonest form was single-edged, triangular in section and tapering evenly from hilt to point, and this form seems to have persisted throughout the knife's history. Sometimes it became quadrangular at the point as a reinforcement for piercing (Plate 34). Very early it was joined by a double-edged variant, also with an even taper. This form of blade had probably appeared at least as early as 1400. By 1450 the double-edged blade had become widely popular, but by then it was usually slender and of thick diamond section. This latter form, with some variations, continued through the sixteenth century.

Scabbards also varied. Iconographic sources indicate that they were often simple leather cases without metal mounts. Sometimes, however, metal bands for suspension appear, and one early scabbard survives in the National Museum in Copenhagen made entirely of silver with a huge finial at the tip shaped like a flattened sphere. Later scabbards frequently had metal throats and very long metal chapes. Also they frequently had pockets for small auxiliary knives. Contemporary pictures show such little knives in place at least as early as 1416, and they were probably much earlier. They continued to be included on many of the scabbards as long as this form of dagger was worn.

Eared Daggers

The fifth of the great families of medieval daggers developed in Spain, probably about the end of the fourteenth century. It was characterized by two discs at the pommel, and these gave the type its modern common name of eared dagger (Plates 36 and 37). The French apparently began to call it an eared dagger (*dague à oreilles*) at least as early as the sixteenth century. At other times they described it as 'in the Spanish fashion'. In Italy it was known as *alla Levantina* because of its Eastern appearance.

The inspiration of the eared dagger was indeed Eastern. As early as the Bronze Age eared daggers of remarkably similar form were made in Persia, and the eared form remained popular for both swords and daggers around the eastern end of the Mediterranean. As far as western Europe was concerned, the form appeared first in the Iberian peninsula. From there it spread, principally to Italy, but also to France, Germany, and England during the fifteenth century. The earliest iconographic representation of it known to the writer is a painting of the martyrdom of St Catherine believed to have been done about 1380 in St George Chapel, Padua.

The eared dagger was almost always a dagger of elegance. Very few simple and unadorned specimens are known. These handsome knives were decorated with enamelling, incised and coloured designs in the bone or ivory grip plaques, etching and damascening in gold and silver, niello work, and finally, in the sixteenth century, cast medallions. Perhaps because of this richness, the eared dagger has been very popular with modern forgers of antique weapons, and the collector must be especially wary when seeking to acquire this form of dagger.

Bashford Dean has suggested in his classic *Catalogue of European Daggers* that one good guide to the period of an eared dagger is the design of the ears themselves. As a rule these ears were formed in one piece with the thick tang of the blade, and often they were covered on their exterior surfaces with plaques of bone, ivory, horn or metal. In the beginning the ears of the hilt were usually almost parallel with each other and with the axis of the hilt. During the second half of the fifteenth century the ears became widely divergent, and in the sixteenth century they diverged even further, sometimes at an angle of 140 degrees or 150 degrees. By 1550 the divergence had reached 160 degrees or even more, so that the ears were almost perpendicular to the grips.

The guard of the eared dagger also underwent a considerable evolution. Pictorial sources indicate that the early fifteenth century eared daggers in Spain possessed ample disc guards similar to those on rondel daggers. As the years passed this guard became smaller, until it was a vestigial spindle by the end of the century, scarcely larger in diameter than the grips themselves and utterly useless as a guard. Sometimes this spindle was a separate piece of metal; sometimes it was an integral forging with the blade and tang, and sometimes it was built up with plaques of bone, ivory, or a similar material that continued up to form the sides of the grips.

The grips were ample in the early fifteenth century types, but became more slender in later years. A few specimens are known with metal grips forged in one piece with the blade and pommel. The usual form, however, consisted of two plaques or scales riveted to the broad tang of the blade. As noted above, these plaques sometimes included both the spindle guard and the outer facings of the ears.

The blade of the typical eared dagger was broad and double-edged. In the very earliest specimens single-edged blades might be found, but these seem to have disappeared early in the fifteenth century. The usual blade also had a heavy ricasso next to the hilt, and this was normally ground irregularly (Plate 38). That is, one side is apt to be longer than the other. The ricasso area is sometimes damascened in arabesques or scroll work, and this decoration may carry up over the guard and along the sides of the tang. The edges of the blade are sometimes hollow ground, sometimes flat. Fifteenth- and early sixteenth-century blades are apt to be slightly leaf-shaped in outline, but narrower straight blades of a thick diamond section are also frequently encoutered (Plate 39).

Scabbards for the eared dagger, like those for many other medieval daggers, are very rare. It is known, however, that the earliest types, for those daggers with large rondel guards, were shaped exactly like the contemporary scabbards for rondel daggers. That is, there was a large circular mouth that came up over the guard. These scabbards seem usually to have been made entirely of leather without any metal mounts. The so-called dagger of Boabdil, last Nasrid King of Granada, in the Real Armeria, however, has both metal throat and tip. If this attribution is correct, as seems likely, it must date before 1492. Later, scabbards for the blade only were also sometimes completed by a metal chape which was often decorated to match the hilt. In some instances there were places for small auxiliary knives.

The great period of popularity for the eared dagger was the hundred years from 1450 to 1550. Earlier, although it was used principally in Spain, it was not confined to that country by any means. After 1550 it began to drop out of existence, though there is one picture of an eared dagger, cited by Bashford Dean in his *Catalogue of European Daggers,* that dates from 1672.

Daggers Popularly Called Cinquedeas

The last of the major families of medieval daggers to develop was that now popularly called the cinquedea (Plate 40). Actually it is a misnomer. The words *cinque diti* mean five fingers in Italian, and arms historians were quick to identify the term with an Italian weapon that had a blade about five fingers wide at the hilt. According to Florio, who published his *New World of Words* in 1611 and so was close to the weapon itself, it referred to a very short Venetian dagger that had a blade only five fingers long. Also the word seems to have been used primarily in the second half of the sixteenth century, after the big broad-bladed type now called by the name had disappeared. Popular usage has now made the meaning so universal, however, that it is used here despite its inaccuracy.

The earliest date to which the weapons now called cinquedeas can be assigned is the middle of the fifteenth century. From their first appearance they continued to develop until about 1490. Thereafter they entered their golden period until 1520 and then swifly disappeared. Unlike other medieval daggers, which enjoyed a wide area of popularity, the cinquedea was confined almost entirely to the Italian peninsula, and primarily to the northern part at that. It had other peculiarities as well. For one thing, in some instances it was a large weapon with a blade of sword length. In others it was a dagger with an 8- to 10-inch blade. It seemingly sprang into use in an almost fully developed state. Such evolution as there was during the late fifteenth and early sixteenth centuries concerned decoration and minor details. For the cinquedea this decoration was exceedingly important. Only the eared dagger approached it in luxury. Specimens were often highly decorated with etching, engraving, gilding, bluing, damascening and carving. Plain examples are almost non-existent. Possibly because of this decoration, the cinquedea, like the eared dagger, has attracted the attention of the faker. This is especially true of the nineteenth century forger of antique arms. Probably no other form of dagger has been so widely counterfeited.

The principal characteristic of the cinquedea is its blade. In the earliest identified specimens this blade tapers evenly from hilt to point. It is also flat in cross-section with a strongly defined median ridge. Well before 1500, however, a form of fluting developed that soon came to be almost universal for the type. This fluting was arranged in three horizontal rows across the blade, with the flutes running with the axis of the blade. Normally there were two flutes near the point, three in the row immediately above them and four flutes in the row above that near the hilt. The same arrangement normally held true no matter what the length of the blade. One occasionally encounters a blade with a different fluting arrangement, but it is a rarity. By 1500, also, the points had become slightly more blunt in many instances. During the sixteenth century cinquedea blades were usually enriched with bluing, gilding, and etching and featured scenes from classical mythology, masks, and floral designs or scrolls.

Among cinquedea hilts there were two principal types. One resembled the contemporary sword with a wheel pommel, sword-like grips, through which a narrow tang passed, and quillons which curved towards the blade and terminated in small flat-sided lobes. Often the quillons were cusped in the centre. Arms historians, notably the late Bashford Dean, have attributed this hilt form to Milan, though without having any real evidence for so doing. The second form of hilt was much more common. It featured a broad blade tang which generally followed the shape of the grips and pommel in its outline. These grips were composed of two scales, usually of wood, horn, bone, or ivory, which were fastened in place by rivets passing through the tang. Frequently, these rivets were metal tubes filled with filigree rosettes. In form, most were flat-sided, swelling markedly in the middle and tapering at both ends. In some there was an extra swelling near the pommel, presumably to afford a better hold. Normally the scales continued up to cover the sides of the arched pommel. The top of the pommel was covered with a shaped strip of gilded brass or iron, and the space between the edges of the two grips scales was sometimes filled with strips of gilded brass so that the tang itself was not visible. The quillons were quadrangular in section and curved sharply towards the blade. Sometimes the arms were almost straight, but still they slanted towards the blade. Both curved and straight types were often cuspate in the centre. In the usual construction, they were either made in two pieces or split so that they received the base of the blade. Attempts have been made to classify cinquedeas with this second form of hilt into types associated with Verona, Ferrara, and Venice, but the divisions are not clear cut, if, indeed, they are valid, and the usual cinquedea finds itself classed simply as 'north Italian'.

Scabbards for the cinquedea seem normally to have been made of hardened leather or *cuir bouilli,* if one may judge by surviving examples (Plate 41). There are very few iconographic sources that show the big dagger in its sheath. This hardened leather offered a rich ground for embossing, and cinquedea scabbards, like the daggers themselves, were frequently richly decorated. Some also had pockets for small auxiliary knives.

Peasant Knives (*Hauswehren*)

In a far different category from the handsome cinquedeas were the simple knives frequently carried by villagers and peasants. The German writers have called this sort of weapon a *Hauswehre* or 'home defence', and it is shown in use by numerous artists, such as Urs Graf, Albrecht Dürer, and the elder Brueghel. A few actual specimens survive, principally in Swiss museums (Plate 42).

In form, the *Hauswehre* resembled a large butcher knife with a guard. The blade was normally single-edged, with the back and edge nearly parallel, until the edge curved to meet the back at the point. The tang was broad, and the grips were composed of two scales, usually of wood or antler, fastened by stout rivets. Often the grips curved in the direction of the edge as they neared the butt, which was capped either by a simple plate of iron or by a flattening of the tang itself. Some *Hauswehren* had quillons (Plate 43). Some simply had a bolster, made of two iron plates, with a single projection on the knuckle side. They were carried in a plain leather sheath often hung, interestingly enough, on the front at the left side instead of the right, as was more common with the fashionable daggers. Simple as they were, *Hauswehren* were sturdy efficient weapons. They were both a direct offshoot of the scramasax and an ancestor of the bowie and hunting knives of the nineteenth century. They remained in use till the late years of the sixteenth century and possibly into the seventeenth as well.

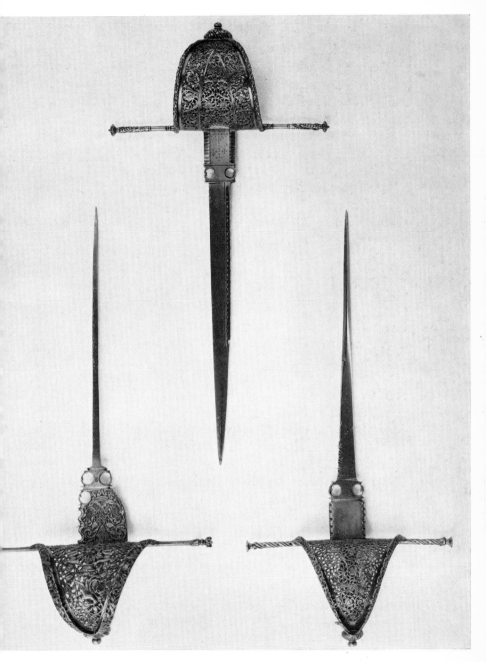

55, 56, 57. Three left-hand daggers of the type called a *main gauche*, Spanish and Italian, mid seventeenth century. *The Wallace Collection, London*

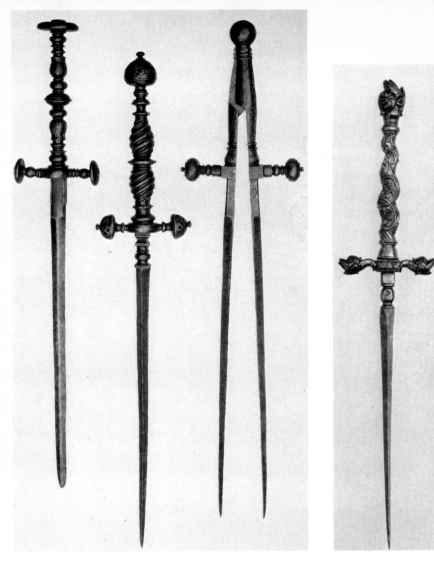

58. (*left*) Stiletto, Italian, mid seventeenth century. *Metropolitan Museum of Art, New York*

59. (*centre*) Stiletto, Italian, mid seventeenth century. *Metropolitan Museum of Art, New York*

60. (*right*) Stiletto made as a pair of dividers, Italian, late seventeenth century. *Metropolitan Museum of Art, New York*

61. (*extreme right*) Stiletto with quillons chiselled as dolphins, Italian, mid seventeenth century. *Metropolitan Museum of Art, New York*

62. Bombardier's stiletto, probably Venetian, mid seventeenth century. *Author's collection*

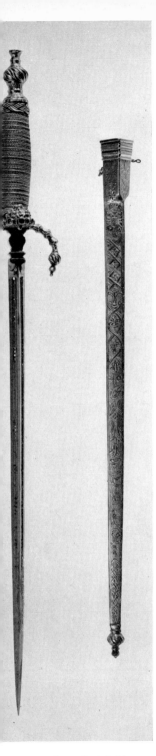

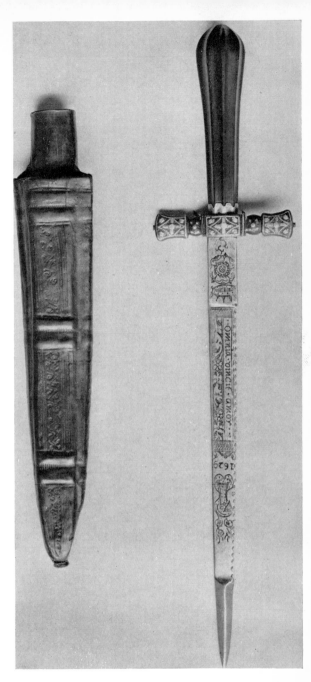

64. English dagger dated 1629. The russeted quillons are encrusted with silver. *Victoria and Albert Museum, London*

63. So-called Schiavona dagger, Venetian or Dalmatian, early eighteenth century. The hilt is silver gilt decorated with pastes; the sheath also is silver gilt. *Tower of London*

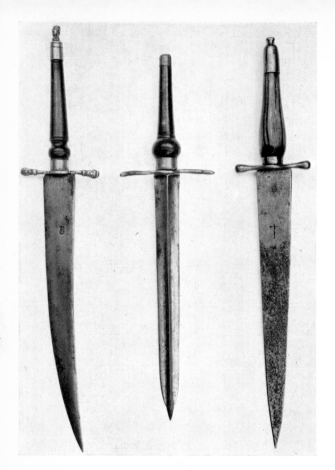

65. (*left*) Plug bayonet bearing the
marks of the London Cutlers
Company. The grip is of
horn, and the brass pommel
and quillon terminals are
fashioned as helmeted heads.
Author's collection

66. (*centre*) Plug bayonet with a
blade triangular in section,
possibly made from a cut
down sword. The handle is
wood, the mounts brass.
Author's collection

67. (*right*) Plug bayonet bearing
the mark of the London
Cutlers Company. The handle
is wood and the mounts brass.
Author's collection

68. Elaborate plug bayonet for
hunting, Spanish, *c.* 1770. The
hilt and sheath mounts are of
steel chiseled and gilt. The
hilt bears the mark of Jacobus
Lavau of Madrid. *Victoria
and Albert Museum, London*

69. (*left*) Scottish dirk with pewter hilt and blade made from a cut down sword, early eighteenth century. *Author's collection*

70. (*above*) Scottish dirk of the fully developed form, mid eighteenth century, with brass mounts. The auxiliary knife and fork are later, dating from about 1782. *Scottish United Services Museum, Edinburgh Castle*

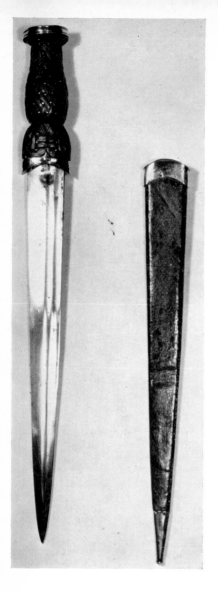

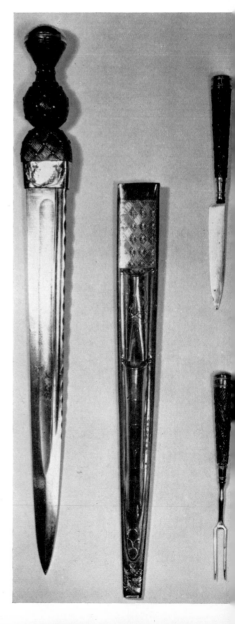

71. Scottish dirk with early form of the balluster handle, *c.* 1775. It is silver mounted and bears the name of Capt. Angus McDonald, 84th Regiment, a unit that was raised in 1775 and disbanded in 1784. *Scottish United Services Museum, Edinburgh Castle*

72. Scottish dirk of degenerate form, *c.* 1815–25. The rosewood handle is exaggerated in form, and the interlace carving has become basket work. The mounts are of gilded brass, and the scabbard bears the mark of the maker, G. Hunter & Co., 25 Princes Street, Edinburgh. *Scottish United Services Museum, Edinburgh Castle*

73. Mediterranean dirk, Italian, *c.* 1725–50. The handle is carved horn. *Metropolitan Museum of Art, New York*

74. Mediterranean dirk with single-edged blade and horn grip with silver mounts, probably Italian, eighteenth century. *Metropolitan Museum of Art, New York*

75. Mediterranean dirk with pierced double-edged blade, probably Italian, late eighteenth century. The horn handle is mounted in silver and decorated with engraved and relief ornament. *Metropolitan Museum of Art, New York*

76. Mediterranean dirk with chiselled and engraved double-edged blade, Sardinian, *c.* 1800. The horn handle is mounted in silver. *Metropolitan Museum of Art, New York*

77. American dagger of the eighteenth century. The quillons are iron; the bands around the wooden grip are pewter. *Leonard D. Pelton Collection*

78. Blade of American rifleman's knife excavated near Fort Ticonderoga. *Author's collection*

79. American rifleman's knife of a type that could have been used in the eighteenth century. *Robert Albrecht Collection*

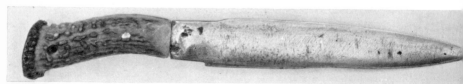

Wood Knife (Trousse de Chasse; Weidpraxe)

One other form of sheath knife was frequently carried during the Middle Ages and later during the Renaissance and in early modern times: this was the wood knife. It was a great-bladed cleaver implement, used by huntsmen for jointing carcasses. It was not a weapon and so deserves little comment here. It will be treated thoroughly in another volume of this series devoted to hunting weapons. Suffice it to say that the blade of the wood knife often expanded toward the blunt or squared point. The edge was chisel-like to cut through bone and cartilage. The tang was broad, and the grips were composed of two scales riveted in place. There was a butt and frequently a butt-cap, but almost never a pommel. Guards were rare, and usually found on very late specimens. This hunting knife was usually carried in a leather scabbard which also contained pockets for a host of smaller knives, knife-sharpeners, and sometimes skewers and forks. There also were tools for bleeding game, skinning and butchering the carcass. The wood knife was only just beginning to assume its characteristic form in the fifteenth century. Its great period of development lay in the next two hundred years.

In addition to the great families of daggers described above, there were also a great many other medieval daggers and fighting knives. Some do not fit readily into any category, as they reflect the individual taste of their owner or maker. There are also two dagger terms used frequently during the Middle Ages that defy identification in spite of the best efforts of modern students. One term is 'misericorde'. Traditionally, a knight used a misericorde to dispatch a wounded adversary or to threaten one with death unless he surrendered. The word appears in both English and French texts of the fourteenth century and occasionally in the fifteenth century. It may have been used to designate any knightly dagger, but arms historians are still unsure. A second common term is 'anlace' or 'anelace'. It appears primarily in English texts and is even earlier than 'misericorde'. For a time students tried to associate the word with the baselard and then, jumping widely, with the so-called cinquedea. Neither can be correct. The etymology of the word suggests that it meant a narrow piercing dagger, but that is all that can be deduced. There is still considerable room left for research in the field of medieval daggers.

Chapter Three

The Sixteenth Century

The sixteenth century brought many changes to the history of the dagger and fighting knife. This was the century in which the sword began to become an important part of civilian costume. In the opening years the dagger was still uniformly carried, often as the only weapon, but after about 1530 the sword was often worn. by knights and gentlemen as part of their normal civilian dress. For them the dagger, if indeed they wore one at all, had become primarily an adjunct of the longer weapon. Peasants and burghers continued to carry a knife when they carried any weapon, but they, too, more and more frequently went unarmed. The medieval emphasis on form and simplicity also gave way to a preference for surface ornamentation. Etched decoration, which had already appeared on cinquedea blades, continued in use. Damascening became more frequent on both blade and handles, as did encrustations of silver and gold on guards, pommels, and scabbard mounts. Relief ornament also increased in favour for hilts and sheaths and, towards the end of the century, a new blade decoration appeared in the form of ornamental piercings.

Forms and types of dagger also began to change. The eared dagger and the cinquedea were still in use as the century opened, but their popularity soon declined. As noted previously, the rondel dagger became decadent, losing its lower rondel early and soon disappearing. Other weapons such as the ballock knife and the Swiss dagger continued through most of the century, but with marked alterations, and most changed of all were the quillon daggers, offering almost a new type in the left-hand daggers at the close of the period. Finally, there was also an entirely new form in the so-called Landsknecht daggers of central Europe.

Ballock Knives

There were two principal forms of the ballock knife during the sixteenth century. One followed the old, generally phalliform, pattern in its hilt; the other boasted a hilt with grips that swelled towards the pommel so that they almost resembled an inverted cone. In these latter cases the pommel consisted solely of a flat metal plate covering the end of the grips. Both of these hilt forms had been in use during most of the medieval period, but the forms became more exaggerated in the sixteenth century.

The phalliform hilts became attenuated to a considerable degree. The grips were long, almost columnar, sometimes fluted. and frequently faceted. The sides were generally parallel. The globes at the base became smaller, but drooped down along the sides of the blade so that the lower line of the hilt became sharply crescentic. This, too, added to the length of the hilt. The pommel end was frequently bulbous and sometimes conical in form, but there are a few surviving examples of this period with almost no pommel at all. In all cases the hilt from pommel to globes at the base was made in one piece, though there was usually a shaped washer between the hilt and the blade. These hilts were still usually made of wood, though at least one specimen with an agate handle still survives (*Historisches Museum*, Basel). In almost all of these late ballock knives the blades were slender, double-edged, and so thickly diamond-shaped in cross-section that they could almost be considered four sided. In some instances there was a flat ricasso, at least between the basal protuberances of the hilt.

One special form of this sort of ballock knife developed about 1500 or shortly before in the area bordering the Baltic Sea, where it was called a *pooke, poeke,* or *poicke.* It was characterized by a phalliform hilt, often with a conical pommel and usually without the sharply crescentic base. Most noticeable was its short, broad single-edged blade. Frequently the blade was only a trifle longer than the hilt, so that it tapered sharply from base to point.

Except for the shape of the grips, the ballock knives with the flat pommel plates generally followed the same form as those with phalliform hilts. Here again, however, there was an exception in the Baltic area. In these northern examples the blades were usually single-edged, and the basal globes were placed on stems so that they became in effect short quillons with spherical finials. In these various forms the ballock daggers continued in use throughout the sixteenth century. By 1600, however, their manufacture was confined to a few very conservative areas. Notable among them was Scotland.

Swiss Daggers

Before 1500 the Swiss dagger had taken form in its basic concepts as an outgrowth of the baselard. The metal-shod crosses at both ends of the grips had assumed their characteristic curved shapes. All that remained were refinements in the shape of the grips and blade and most especially in the design of the scabbards. Also in the fully evolved form there developed the practice of inserting iron or brass washers between the metal portions of the upper and lower crosses and the wooden part of the hilt. These changes had all occurred before 1515, by which date fully developed dagger appears in a number of paintings.

The shape of the grips of the sixteenth-century Swiss dagger was quite different from its fifteenth-century predecessor. Instead of the slender straight-sided form that had characterized the type since its earliest days in the baselard family, the Swiss daggers developed relatively broad grips with slightly convex edges and a low median ridge down both of the broader sides. These grips were normally made of one piece of dark hardwood, drilled for the tang of the blade. The transition to the crosses at top and bottom were graceful and often slightly curved. The sides of the crosses, however, were flat, not rounded as they had been earlier. Variations exist in a series of de luxe daggers boasting metal hilts completely covered with relief decorations. Often these hilts followed the general lines of the more usual Swiss dagger, but sometimes the grips became vase-shaped, and the crosses varied widely.

The blade also assumed a new form. The even taper that had been typical of the fifteenth century specimens gave way to a slightly leaf-shaped blade that tapered from hilt to point in a convex line. Blades were almost always double-edged and diamond-shaped in cross-section, so that there was a distinct line running down the centre. There were, of course, a few variations in blades that offer exceptions to the general rule. Specimens survive with straight sides, suddenly narrowed and reinforced points, with grooves instead of a central ridge and occasionally with piercings, but all such aberrations are extremely rare. Almost always these blades were completely plain, no matter how decorative the mounts and scabbards.

Perhaps the most noticeable of all the Swiss dagger's characteristics, however, was its scabbard. At first this was a simple affair made of two pieces of wood covered with leather and mounted with a metal throat and chape. By 1510, however, the metal mounts began to expand in size and complexity until the entire front of the sheath was covered in brass or silver and frequently gilded. This metal covering was highly decorated with cast and pierced designs, often further enhanced by engraving. The leading Swiss artists of the period lent their talent to designing decorative scabbards for the national dagger. Most famous was Hans Holbein the Younger, and indeed Swiss daggers have sometimes been called 'Holbein daggers' because of his association with them. His most famous designs were prepared between 1523 and 1540. Urs Graf was perhaps the first of the artists to turn to scabbard designing, producing designs in 1511 and 1512, while Heinrich Aldegraver and Peter Flötner also offered their talents to the task during the first half of the century.

Some few of the surviving drawings indicate that Swiss dagger sheaths were occasionally designed to be viewed in a vertical position. These drawings, especially by Graf and Aldegraver, show scabbards completely sheathed in metal, bearing relief ornaments of floral sprays and scrolls, medallions, putti, nude figures, and sometimes scenes from the Bible or mythology. By far the majority of designs and almost all the surviving examples, however, present sheaths intended to be viewed in a horizontal position. Decorations are almost always based on the Bible, mythology, legend, or history. The Dance of Death and the William Tell story were especially popular. Occasionally a lily or cross is featured. Because Holbein's drawings are the earliest to show the sheath designed for a horizontal orientation, he is often considered to have originated it. There is, however, no real proof that he did so. The popularity of the scabbard with metal mounts depicting such scenes in a horizontal fashion reached its height between 1540 and 1560, and it continued until the end of of the century. The latest dated specimen known to survive stems from the year 1592. It is now in the Victoria and Albert Museum, London (Plate 44). A few of the sheaths were equipped with small auxiliary knives or sharpening steels, but most were not.

The Swiss dagger was widely popular in its native territory. It was worn by both patrician and *Landsknecht*. As might be expected from the orientation of the scabbard decoration, the dagger was normally worn in a horizontal position so that the scenes would be viewed in an upright position. Actually it was undoubtedly the method of wearing the dagger that suggested the alignment of the decorative scenes. Occasionally the weapon seems to have been worn on the right side, but most often it was carried at the back with the hilt to the wearer's right.

Quillon Daggers

The most widely popular of all dagger families in the fifteenth century were those with quillons. In one form or another they were carried in all parts of Europe throughout the entire period. They picked up where the medieval quillon daggers had left off, and they gave way in turn to other forms in the seventeenth century. They were worn by the aristocracy and by the middle class, when in armour or civilian dress. They were worn in almost every manner that daggers had been previously, and they were used in a number of ways. The downward stabbing blow remained predominant for the greater part of the century, but about mid-century a new fighting technique brought forth the left-hand dagger and a new method of employment that will be described below.

The quillon dagger of the sixteenth century came in a great variety of forms and sizes. For the most part, the direct copies of contemporary sword hilts had disappeared, although some daggers were definitely made *en suite* with swords, offering matched pommels, quillon terminals, and decoration. By and large, however, sword guards were becoming too complicated for mimicking in a smaller weapon. There were quillon daggers without pommels as well as with them, and the quillons themselves might be curved, straight, short, or long. Blades might be single- or double-edged, flat or almost quadrangular. There was little uniformity.

There is, however, one special type of quillon dagger of the early 1500s that can be classified. It seems to have been most popular in Germany and Austria, and collectors have frequently given it the name of Maximilian dagger (Plate 45). This weapon is characterized by a fluted pommel and quillon terminals. Some pommels are a flat mushroom shape, some are spherical, and in the latter case the fluting is normally spiral. The quillon terminals in either case are normally spherical and spirally fluted. Occasionally one encounters a flat quillon, but these are rare, and always the guard is short. Also both pommel and guard are normally iron. The grips are normally of wood, sometimes covered with leather. They may be made in two zones like those of a hand-and-a-half sword with a ring separating them, or they may be smooth and slightly convex, or they may even be carved as a series of squares or triangles laid on top of each other with the angles projecting alternately. Blades are almost always double-edged and taper evenly from hilt to point. Most often they are flat with a distinct median ridge, but slightly diamond-shaped cross-sections are also known. Such daggers as these date primarily from the first quarters of the sixteenth century. They are scarce, after 1525 and rare after 1540.

A second, though much smaller, group of quillon daggers can also be isolated from Italy during the first half of the sixteenth century. This class of dagger is characterized by a pommel shaped in outline like a vase or fig, but with flat sides and usually decorated in relief with floral sprays and tendrils and masks (Plate 46). The short quillons curve forward towards the blade and are often ornamented with acanthus leaves and other floral ornaments and winged masks. In some examples they terminate in fish, serpent or monster heads. Quite often both pommel and guard are cast in bronze. The grips are usually wrapped with braided wire. Most characteristic of all, however, are the broad double-edged blades that taper evenly from base to point. One side of these blades is usually flat or slightly thickened in the middle, with a low median ridge; the other is fluted or faceted in a series of four of five transverse zones. Because the flaring pommel and tapering grips have reminded some viewers of a fish tail, these daggers have sometimes been called fish-tail daggers, notably by the late Bashford Dean. Sir Guy Laking, on the other hand, ranked them as a modification of the cinquedea. The relatively broad faceted blade and the short curved quillons are indeed somewhat reminiscent of the cinquedea, but it would seem that the daggers do represent a small but separate class.

Both of these types, as well as all of the individual variation of the quillon dagger in the first half of the century, were mere preludes to the really important development which occurred after about 1550. This was the appearance of the so-called left-hand dagger (Plate 47). Such weapons were designed to be held in the left hand like a short-sword, while the rapier was clutched in the right. In the school of fence which brought this dagger into being the opponents faced each other almost directly head on and attacked and parried with both hands simultaneously. The rapier was primarily the attack weapon, while the dagger was used to parry the enemy's rapier or possibly to attack if an opportunity should present itself.

In order to fulfil its functions as a parrying arm, the left-hand dagger needed stout quillons. Such quillons also served better if they were long. Often they were bent forward sharply towards the blade in the hope than an opponent's blade might be caught between quillon and blade and held tight by a slight turning motion of the wrist. If this could be done, it would immobilize the enemy's attacking weapon and leave the duellist free to concentrate on his own offensive movements. Quillons designed for this purpose start out at right-angles to the blade, then curve forward until their distal ends are actually parallel to the axis of the weapon and perhaps an inch and a quarter or an inch and a half from the edge. Sometimes they bent forward at the same time to offer another opportunity for trapping a sword blade. Other left-hand daggers boast quillons that curve toward the blade on one end only, with the other end curving up over the knuckles in the beginning of a knuckle-bow (Plate 48). Since all left-hand daggers were made *en suite* with a rapier of one form or another, the terminals of their quillons almost always duplicated those of the sword with which they were mated. They might be square, rounded, cusped, or equipped with a tiny finial, plain or covered with silver or gold, but always they matched the sword for which they were made.

Another interesting feature of the guard of a left-hand dagger was the ring or shell that normally appeared on one side of the quillons as they crossed the grips. This device was so placed that it served as a protection for the knuckles when the dagger was held in the proper position. If an opponent's rapier were parried and slid down the blade of the parrying dagger, it would come to rest on this ring or shell and stop there. Without such a supplementary guard, it would strike directly into the holder's knuckles and perhaps disable that hand.

Like the quillon terminals, the pommels also matched those on the rapiers with which the individual left-hand daggers were paired. Some were spherical, some ovoid, some squarish, vase-shaped or cylindrical. Some were smooth, some fluted. Decorations on both pommels and guards also varied with gilding chiselling, enamelling, gold and silver damascening or encrustations and etching being among the most popular types of enrichment. Since these were fighting weapons, not just dress adornments, and since the guards were designed to receive the full weight of an opponent's blow if necessary, almost all pommels and guards were made of iron. Only the enrichments were created from other metals.

The blades found in left-hand daggers varied somewhat, but primarily they were straight and double-edged with a strong ricasso at the hilt. The basic form of most afforded an even taper from ricasso to point and a diamond shape in cross-section. The ricasso was normally flat and straight-sided with a depression for the thumb on the side opposite the ring guard. The better-quality blades, however, were far from simple (Plate 49). They were ridged, grooved, and pierced in both simple and intricate patterns with holes in the form of circles, squares, diamonds, and crosses. Formerly, it was the romantic notion of many collectors that this piercing and grooving was designed to hold poisons. Actually, the ribbing and thickness of the blade were designed to afford rigidity for parrying and thrusting, and the grooves and piercings were added principally to reduce the weight and keep the weapon light and well balanced. A secondary factor was decoration in the simple types, and actually ornamentation probably became a major consideration in the more elaborate specimens, for after all a simply bored round hole would reduce weight as efficiently as a complex series of diamonds and crosses which had to be both drilled and filed.

Two rare forms of blade were also produced. Both were designed to entrap an opponent's sword blade. One had deep serrations along one side, so that the spaces between them stuck out like teeth (Plate 51). It is often called a sword-breaker blade. The other was divided longitudinally into three parts which folded together to resemble a conventional blade (Plate 50).

When a spring was released, however, they flew apart to form a sort of trident. Both of these blade types were late, dating from about 1600, almost at the end of the left-hand dagger's popularity.

Since this form of dagger was designed to be held in the left hand like a miniature sword with the blade above the hand, one would expect that it would have been worn on the right side towards the front or perhaps horizontally across the back with the hilt to the left. In many instances it was carried in just these positions, but contemporary illustrations show that it was also carried vertically on the left side and horizontally across the back with the hilt to the right, so that it could not possibly have been drawn with the left hand. Scabbards were normally of wood, covered with leather and mounted with iron lockets and chapes. These metal portions were usually decorated *en suite* with the hilts of the daggers which they held.

As noted above, the left-hand dagger developed in the middle of the sixteenth century. It reached its height about 1590 and continued into the seventeenth, where it was joined by another form, popular in Spain and Italy. These later forms will be discussed in the next chapter.

Landsknecht Daggers

The ballock knife, the Swiss dagger, and the quillon daggers all represented forms that had begun well before the sixteenth century. The *Landsknecht* dagger was entirely a product of that century. In reality the term is a modern one, used to indicate any of three specific forms of dagger that became popular with the foot soldiers of Germany and Switzerland during the sixteenth century.

The first form of dagger that is normally designated by the name *Landsknecht* today appeared about 1500 or very shortly thereafter. It is immediately recognizable by its guard, which resembled that on the contemporary short *Landsknecht* sword or *Katzbalger* (Plate 52). The long quillons are S-shaped, bending around so tightly that they give the appearance of a circular guard at first glance. Normally they terminate in ball finials and usually they are decorated with roping. The blades are normally double-edged and taper evenly from hilt to point. The grips are made of wood, bone, or ivory without covering, and the pommels flare like those of the *Landsknecht* sword. The period of use of these miniature *Katzbalgers* was short, perhaps no longer than the first quarter of the century, and they are very rare today.

The second type of *Landsknecht* dagger was used for a much longer time and was much more popular. Some students consider it a derivative of the late rondel dagger. It was characterized by an all-metal hilt that usually flared upwards from guard to pommel, so that the grips became a sort of inverted cone (Plate 53). The pommel itself was sometimes a flat cap, sometimes slightly convex. The grips were frequently ribbed horizontally so that they appeared to be made of a series of thick rings. Sometimes they were ribbed spirally. The guard was a flat plate, lobed, and bent towards the blade. Often there were three lobes, two serving as quillons, and a third, bigger than the others, in the centre on the obverse side, serving as an additional guard. The blade was straight and double-edged with an even taper. Most characteristic of all, however, was the massive scabbard, which was circular in cross-section and heavily mounted in iron. Sometimes the entire surface was metal. Usually it was divided into zones by a series of two or three prominent mouldings, and often the tip of the chape enlarged as a wide disc to parallel the pommel of the dagger.

The third form of dagger that is sometimes called *Landsknecht* by collectors today resembles the common type only in its heavy cylindrical scabbard with wide metal mounts that frequently featured raised mouldings (Plate 54). The hilt of the dagger was entirely different. The guard usually consisted of short quillons and a side-ring similar to those on left-hand daggers. The grips were usually wrapped with twisted wire, and the pommels might be urn-shaped, pear-shaped, or inverted cones. Unlike the popular *Landsknecht* type, which was usually quite plain, these daggers were often enriched with silver overlays and etching on the metal mounts of the sheath and on the guard and pommel. These daggers date from the last quarter of the sixteenth century and they were made primarily in eastern Germany, especially Saxony. They had no vogue in any other part of Europe. For this reason they are also loosely called Saxon daggers or, more accurately, Saxon daggers of *Landsknecht* form. They ceased to be used very soon after 1600, so that their period of popularity was quite short. The combination of their rarity and the fine decoration that was normally applied to them has made these weapons very attractive to collectors and thus quite expensive when they appear upon the market. Despite this situation, few of these Saxon types have been faked, though unscrupulous workmen have added extra decoration to some of the plainer specimens in an effort to increase their value. It is a characteristic of sixteenth-century daggers in general that the richness of the surface decoration applied to many of them invites such fraud.

Chapter Four

The Seventeenth Century

In the sixteenth century knives and daggers had begun to lose their cultural significance as the sword became more important. The seventeenth century brought a further decline in the importance of the dagger. Both the number and the variety of knives and daggers diminished, and they were carried by fewer people. In northern Europe knives and daggers were worn for special purposes and occasions, but they had ceased to be an important adjunct of civilian costume for everyday use. In southern Europe, especially Italy, daggers were much more common. The left-hand dagger, which had begun to disappear in northern areas in the third decade of the century, continued in the form of the *main gauche* as an important weapon in Spain and Italy. Stilettos appeared in a variety of forms and achieved widespread popularity in Italy. Special daggers also appeared in England and Scotland. Most important of all, from the standpoint of arms history, the bayonet developed in southern France. It appeared early in the century and in succeeding years it spread over most of Europe to become almost universal for military use before 1700.

Left-hand Daggers

The northern form of left-hand dagger continued with little or no change during the first twenty years of the seventeenth century. The only clue to the date consists usually of slight differences in the decoration, which, in some instances, begin to reflect the baroque taste, but even this is frequently absent. But the left-hand dagger in its quillon style was gradually dropping from favour. It disappeared completely during the third decade of the century.

Much more important was the southern form of left-hand

dagger which modern collectors usually call by its French name, *main gauche* (Plates 55, 56 and 57). This dagger began to appear in Spain, in the Spanish Netherlands, and in the portion of Italy under Spanish domination just as the older type vanished. Normally it was a bigger weapon, with a longer and heavier blade and very long straight quillons. Most characteristic of all, however, was the wide guard that curved from the quillons to the pommel and protected the holder's knuckles. In almost all instances this guard was triangular in outline, though some lobed and domed shapes and other symmetrical forms are known. Usually also the edges of this guard were turned over outwards, possibly to trap the point of an opponent's blade and prevent it from slipping off into the holder's hand or wrist. The base of this triangular guard was either made in one with the quillons, or welded or riveted to them. The apex usually hooked into a hole in the pommel.

Since this style of dagger was usually made *en suite* with a cup-hilted rapier, the decoration of the knuckle guard paralleled that of the cup of the rapier. The better ones were pierced and chiselled in finely wrought openwork designs, featuring floral scrolls and traceries. These were produced by drilling and filing the holes, then chiselling and chasing the designs. Since these daggers have often been the subject of forgers, the collector should beware of any specimen that has been cast instead of wrought and of any piece that shows burrs along the inside of the piercings. Embossed decoration is also highly suspect. Simpler guards are often completely plain or have only a few chased lines for decoration.

The quillons are normally cylindrical with knobbed tips. In many examples they are decorated with spiral fluting, usually including a chased leaf design in alternate flutes. Other quillon decorations are also occasionally met. The chief feature of the quillons, however, is their length, which is often 11 ins., or even more from tip to tip.

Pommels are globular, usually flattened at top and bottom and with a button at the top. Normally they are decorated to match the quillons and are direct, though smaller, copies of the pommels of their matching rapiers. Occasionally one encounters a hollow pommel with pierced decorations, but authentic ones are rarities.

Grips are normally made of wood and wrapped with twisted and braided wire. Many have a spiral pattern in the wood beneath the wrappings. Some daggers of this form are known, however, with cylindrical metal grips pierced with patterns similar to those on the knuckle guard.

Blades are long and stout, and usually they are made in three distinct zones. The first zone, next to the hilt, comprises the ricasso, which may be as much as 3 ins. long. It is flat-sided and slightly bevelled at the edges. At its forward end there is frequently either one large hole or two slightly smaller ones. In some examples there are also two arms running parallel to the sides of the ricasso and separated from it by perhaps half an inch. These were designed to catch the blade of the opponent's rapier in much the same fashion as the curved quillons of the northern type of left-hand dagger. On the side of the ricasso opposite the knuckle guard there is usually an oval depression for the thumb. The second section of the blade is normally single-edged and formed like a flat triangle in cross-section. The edge faces the holder's left when the dagger is grasped in its functional position. The back of the blade in this section is usually filed with a series of grooves or notches. The final, and by far the longest, section of the blade stretches from this single-edged portion to the point. It normally comprises slightly more than half the total length of the blade, and is double-edged with a diamond cross-section. Occasionally it will have notches or serrations for a short distance along its edge which corresponds to the back of the previous zone. Total lengths of 19 ins. or even slightly more are not unusual for these dagger blades. The three-zoned blade is the most usual of all, but it is not the only one that is found. Sometimes the intermediate zone between the ricasso and point is omitted; sometimes the proportion between the three is varied, and in rare instances the blade narrows suddenly at the forward end of the ricasso and becomes almost a stiletto with a thick diamond cross-section.

The Spanish form of left-hand dagger appeared in the second quarter of the seventeenth century. It reached its peak of development in the third quarter, and thereafter entered a period of decline, although it actually continued in use until the late eighteenth century. Spain was a conservative country, and the cup-hilted rapier remained in use there well after the small-sword had supplanted it in most of the rest of Europe. While the long rapier continued in fashion the left-hand dagger accompanied it. The later specimens, however, are usually plain, the quillons and blades are apt to be shorter, and the knuckle guards lose their even curve from quillons to pommel and become boxy.

Stilettos

Although the stiletto or stylet may have developed during the late years of the sixteenth century, it is typically a weapon of the seventeenth century. Certainly it was only after 1600 that it became fully developed. The earliest stilettos may have derived from the left-hand daggers of the northern type. At least some typical parrying daggers are known with slender stabbing blades of triangular or rectangular section, and since the left-hand dagger is an earlier form, it is tempting to think that the evolution may have come from that direction. There is, however, no proof, and no definite evolutionary series exists. Except for a very few stilettos with parrying hilts, the form with all its characteristics seems almost to have sprung into existence full-blown and achieved instant popularity. It was primarily an Italian weapon, and was probably developed in the northern area of the Italian peninsula, where it achieved its greatest popularity.

The typical stiletto was a short light stabbing weapon (Plates 58 and 59). A few specimens as long as 19 or 20 ins. are known, but they are exceptions. Many are as short as 9 or 10 ins., and a few are even shorter. The blade is normally of a strong piercing form, either rectangular or triangular in section, with a sharp point and no edge whatsoever. On many there is a short baluster-turned section at the base. The hilt is characterized by short quillons which normally terminate in buttons or spheres, though some are sculptured in human or animal forms. In a few instances there is only one quillon instead of two. Pommels may be discoidal, spherical or ovate, or again they may be sculptured to resemble a human, a fish, or an animal (Plate 61). Grips may be wood, bone, or horn, smooth or carved in spirals and sometimes studded with tiny tacks. Most typical, however, are all-metal grips made in one piece with the pommel. These are normally decorated in a variety of fashions with baluster turnings, chiselled patterns, and dozens of other forms. Many are exquisite examples of steel cutting.

Aside from these typical stilettos, there were also special types and variants. One of these was the artillerist's or bombardier's stiletto, which bore a weight scale for cannon balls on its blade (Plate 62). Sometimes this interesting weapon was made with a chiselled steel hilt like the more usual types, but the most common form, which appears to have been made in Venice, had an entirely different hilt. Both pommel and quillon terminals were iron and made in the form of swirled and pointed ovals. The grips were normally horn with a distinct swell in the centre. They were carved spirally and usually wrapped with twisted wires in the grooves of the spirals. Most often they were also studded with tiny nails. The blades were always triangular in cross-section, and the broad side of the blade was marked with a series of numbers, of which the most common was 1, 3, 6, 9, 12, 14, 16, 20, 30, 40, 50, 60, 90, 100, 120. Between each number there was a line, so that the series formed a sort of scale. These numbers correspond with the most popular calibres of cannon used in Italy during the seventeenth century, and it is believed that originally these daggers were designed so that a gunner could measure the bore of a cannon or the diameter of a cannon ball and read the weight of the projectile on this scale. In the beginning this may actually have been the case, but it would seem that the numbers soon became a convention, for most of the surviving examples which the writer has been able to examine differ slightly from each other, and none will actually work as a weight scale. Probably the daggers quickly became a status symbol for artillerymen, and artisans copied them without a full understanding of the purpose of the numbers. A few of the scales offer slightly different numbers and an occasional specimen stops with the number 100. Most, however, go to 120, and for this reason the type is sometimes called a *centoventi*, which means one hundred and twenty in Italian. Normally these artillerist's stilettos were big fighting weapons, suitable for soldiers. Small ones might be 12 ins. long; bigger ones as much as 19 to 20 ins.

Another unusual form of the stiletto was also associated with the military, either artillery men or engineers. It had a split and pivoted blade that could serve as a compass or a pair of dividers (Plate 60).

The exact dating of stilettos as a whole is very difficult. There are almost no contemporary pictures that show them, and documentary references are scarce. To complicate the matter further, almost no specimens are dated or precisely datable. They first appeared after 1600 and seem to have reached their peak of popularity about the middle of the century. Apparently they continued in use for many more years and stilettos of pure form may have been used well into the eighteenth century. This seems entirely likely, but absolute documentation would be very difficult if not impossible. On the other hand, degenerate forms of the stiletto, including the so-called schiavona dagger of Venice and Dalmatia and the peasant stilettos with one quillon of Spain and Italy, were definitely carried well into the eighteenth century (Plate 63).

English Daggers

Shortly after 1600 a distinctive form of quillon dagger appeared in England and it continued popular until at least the third quarter of the century (Plate 64). The quillons of this readily recognizable weapon were shaped, partly round and partly rectangular in section. The portion of the quillons which crossed the blade was normally rectangular, then followed baluster or ball turnings, another squared section, and finally a tiny ball finial on each tip. There were some variations in these forms, but these characteristic elements normally remained. Almost always these quillons were of russeted steel decorated with encrustations of silver. There was a ferrule at the base of the grips, and both grips and pommel were made in one piece. There was, in fact, no true pommel, only a swelling of the grips and a rounded butt. In many ways these one-piece grips and pommel resemble those found on ballock knives of the late sixteenth century. Normally they were made of dense, dark wood and they were often fluted. The blades also were very distictive, usually being divided into three zones. The first zone comprised a squared ricasso followed by a long single-edged section for the second area and tipped by a stoutly reinforced point of thick diamond-section for the final zone. Both of the first two zones were frequently decorated with etched designs and mottoes, and often there was a date. Scabbards were made of hardened leather, usually without metal mounts, though there were often pockets for two smaller knives. Tooled decoration was common. All of the specimens of this type of dagger that the writer has encountered were handsome well-made pieces, obviously designed for persons of wealth. There may have been simple pieces of this form also, but they could not have been common.

Ballock Daggers

Closely allied to the English quillon daggers is a series of ballock-hilted daggers believed, on the evidence of inscriptions found on them, to have been made in southern Scotland or possibly northern England during the first quarter of the seventeenth century. Frequently the wooden one-piece grips and pommel are fluted and almost identical with those on the English quillon daggers. At other times the grips are columnar or faceted, and there are distinct mushroom-shaped pommels, similar to the classic phalliform ballock-dagger hilts of earlier centuries. In all instances the globular swellings at the base of the hilt are small and terminate in a sharply crescentic line across the base of the blade. Normally there is an iron or steel washer between the guard and blade which is fastened to the hilt by two pins that pass through the lobes and end in silver rosettes on the tops of the lobes. The usual woods for the hilts are ebony, ivy root, box, or even thorn.

The blades found in these daggers vary considerably, yet all are immediately recognizable as belonging to the same general family. All bear etched and heavily gilded decorations, consisting primarily of scrollwork and mottoes, though some also have heraldic devices. Most, also, are marked by their makers, though none of these marks has yet been identified. A few are dated, and the range of recorded dates now extends from 1605 until 1624. In shape, all blades taper evenly from hilt to point, all are long and slender, and all are heavily diamond-shaped in section for at least a portion of their length. Here the similarity ends. Some are diamond-sectioned for their entire length. Some have ricassos that may be flat with the apex of the diamond or recessed. Some are hollow ground, some flat ground, and at least one has a recessed flat zone between two areas of diamond section.

Scabbards are of hardened leather or *cuir bouilli*. They are usually tooled in decorative patterns and are almost always generally cylindrical in section. There are no metal mounts, but there are sometimes pockets for an auxiliary knife and a bodkin.

Despite the fact that none of these daggers has been found bearing a date later than 1624, it was suggested by C. A. Whitelaw that daggers of this or a similar form continued in use for a longer period of time and that they are, in fact, the forerunners of the Scottish dirk that appeared about 1650 or 1660 and developed fully in the next century. The relationship between the Scottish dirk and the ballock knife has long been sensed by arms students. The hilt of the dirk with the rudimentary basal lobes and the crescentic line across the base of the blade are immediately apparent as continuing features. Now that the ballock dagger, described above, has definitely been linked to Scotland at a date after such weapons had disappeared from the rest of Europe, the connexion seems almost surely established. Sir Guy Laking first distinguished the type, but it remained for Claude Blair and John Wallace to establish the Scottish connexion by discovering a large number of specimens and noting that the mottoes and heraldic devices found on their blades have, when identifiable, all been related to lowland Scots taste and practice. It remains only to identify the minor transition form between these daggers and the dirk described in the next chapter to complete the evolutionary chain.

Bayonets

The bayonet takes its name from the French city of Bayonne. At least as early as the mid-sixteenth century this city was famous for its daggers, which came to be called *dagues de Bayonne* or *Bayonettes*. At what date these daggers first came to be attached to firearms to form a sort of spear is not known. It may have happened in the late sixteenth century, but it seems more likely that this epoch-making association dates from the first quarter of the seventeenth century, especially since the earliest specific references to the practice appear in the memoirs of the famous French soldier, Marshal Jacques de Puységur, who had written in 1642 that his musketeers were equipped with such weapons so that they could defend themselves 'if anyone wished to come at them after they had fired'. By 1647 there are ample references which indicate that the technique of attaching a dagger haft to the muzzle of a firearm was well known in the vicinity of the bayonet's native city. Puységur, who was also a native of Bayonne, described these first bayonets as having straight double-edged blades a foot long and tapering wooden handles also a foot long. These handles were of a proper diameter for being inserted into the muzzles of muskets, and thus collectors today refer to them as plug bayonets. A later French reference (Gaya's *Traité des Armes* of 1678) described the bayonet as having a blade a foot long and a 'good inch' in width, but by this time the handle had shrunk to a more manageable 8 or 9 ins.

At this juncture the bayonet was gaining rapid acceptance among military men. Some British regiments at Tangiers were armed with it as early as 1663, and the Saxon army also began to use it in that year. Probably the French did also, for there is an edict of Louis XIV, dated 1666, banning the use of the bayonet without royal licence. The terms of the edict, however, suggest that some regiments were being issued bayonets at the time, and the official ban seems to have been of short duration. The new French regiments of fusiliers and grenadiers raised in 1671 were supposedly fully armed with the handy new weapon, and it undoubtedly spread to other regiments as well. The day of the bayonet had dawned, and during the last quarters of the century almost all European nations adopted it as a standard arm.

These plug bayonets came in a variety of shapes and styles (Plates 65, 66 and 67). Blades might be straight and double-edged with diamond or hexagonal sections. They might also be single-edged and shaped like a flat triangle in section. In such instances there was usually a false edge along the back at the point. Some single-edged bayonets had slightly curved blades, especially some of the English types, and a very few plug bayonets had blades that were triangular in section with only vestigal edges and so were useful only for stabbing.

Hilts were more uniform than blades. Normally there were short quillons. In some cases these ended in lobed terminals; in others they were sculptured in the form of human heads or other figures. Above the guard was a ferrule around the base of the grips, which were usually made of wood, horn, bone, or ivory, so that they would fit tightly in the gun muzzle without scarring it. Most of these grips had a pronounced swelling next to the ferrule. Then they tapered evenly in a straight or concave line to the pommel. This pommel was narrow and never projected beyond the diameter of the grips at their juncture. Often it was simply a cap, but in some instances it boasted a sculptural form. One English pattern that seems to have been very popular during the very late seventeenth century, and possibly the opening years of the next century, boasted pommels and quillon terminals in the form of helmeted heads or of cherubs.

The majority of plug bayonets were military weapons, and these were normally quite plain. But bayonets were also used for hunting (Plate 68). With the aid of a bayonet, a sporting gun could be made to serve the same functions as the old boar spear for killing a wounded beast or protecting a hunter from a charging animal when his firearm was unloaded. Bayonets for this purpose were luxury arms made for wealthy sportsmen, and they were often handsomely decorated. Blades were sometimes etched, gilded or even chiselled. Mounts might be chiselled steel or brass cast in sculptural forms and possibly gilt as well. Grips might be striated or even engraved with designs. The bayonets intended for princely bodyguards might rival these hunting weapons in luxury, and it is frequently difficult to determine whether a given bayonet was used for sport or by such a guard. Heraldic devices are often a help in such instances and so, sometimes, is the diameter of the grips, for hunting guns frequently had a smaller bore than the military muskets carried by guards.

As a weapon the plug bayonet had many drawbacks. It was a reasonably good dagger, but difficulties arose when it was attached to the musket. Once it was inserted no shot could be fired until it was removed. If it was pushed in too tightly, it was difficult to remove. If it was not pushed in tightly enough, it might fall out or be left in an enemy's body. Thus means were sought to improve the attachment. Probably about 1678 loose rings were fastened to the grips which could be looped around the gun barrel. They did not work well, however, and their use never became widespread.

Real improvement came with the invention of the socket bayonet a few years later. This bayonet offered a sleeve that fitted around the gun barrel instead of a dagger handle, and it locked in place with a slot and stud arrangement. The great French military engineer Marshal Sebastien le Prestre de Vauban devised such a bayonet in 1687, and, at his urging, it was adopted for the French infantry in 1688. Other nations followed France's example, and an improved version of the socket bayonet became standard for almost all European armies shortly after 1700. With this development the plug bayonet disappeared from the military scene although it remained in use for hunting in Spain throughout the eighteenth and even into the early nineteenth century. There were a few attempts to combine the bayonet and dagger during the eighteenth and nineteenth centuries, notably one of the Baker rifle bayonets of Great Britain at the end of the eighteenth century and the Dahlgren bowie bayonet of the United States in the 1860s, but, in general, bayonet and dagger followed different courses from the disappearance of the plug until the advent of the knife bayonet in the present century, well after the termination of this study.

Chapter Five

The Eighteenth Century

———————— ⟫⟪◆⟫⟪ ————————

By 1700 the wearing of daggers and fighting knives had become restricted to a few specific areas of the Western world. In the cities and among most of the sophisticated areas of western Europe and America the small-sword was the gentleman's weapon. An occasional quillon dagger might be worn for a special purpose or presented as a token of esteem, but these were unusual occurrences. The carrying of knives or daggers as popular items of dress or as customary weapons for personal defence was confined primarily to Scotland where the Highland dirk developed to the countryfolk of Spain and Italy where another dirk became a significant item of dress, and to the frontiers of America where a scalping or butcher knife was both an important weapon and a general tool. There was little change in this situation during the eighteenth century. Patterns of dirks might evolve gradually, but those peoples who were fond of daggers at the beginning of the century still clung to them at its close. No new groups were added to their ranks, but none left them.

Scottish Dirk

The Scottish dirk probably appeared shortly after the middle of the seventeenth century. Actually the earliest dating evidence is supplied by a portrait of an unknown Highlander in the Scottish National Portrait Gallery that is believed to have been painted about 1670, and by a surviving dirk in the National Museum of Antiquities of Scotland, Edinburgh, that is inscribed 'Fear God and do not kill 1680', but it is believed that dirks had been in use for some years earlier. Many students hold that the very first Scottish dirks displayed an affinity to the ballock knife in that they had fully rounded haunches similar to the protuberances at the base of the grips of that earlier dagger. The inscribed specimen mentioned above originally had just such rounded haunches as this, but the dirk in the 1670 portrait, on the other hand, has haunches with the sides flattened in the plane of the blade like the traditional later forms of the weapon. Thus it is evident that the flat-sided form developed very early, if, indeed, it is the second form. Actually both shapes may have appeared simultaneously, though the theory of typological evolution would still seem to indicate that the rounded form came first, since it is closer to an earlier style.

In its other aspects, the Scottish dirk of the late seventeenth century boasted a flat or slightly domed pommel, grips with generally parallel sides, and a single-edged blade that tapered evenly from hilt to point. Often there was also a false edge for some 5 or 6 ins. from the point. Sometimes the grips were covered with fish skin or possibly leather and wrapped with twisted wire, as seems to be the case in the 1670 portrait. More often they appear to have been made of wood, bone, or ivory, with a pattern of turned bands. Sometimes there were carved bands of triple interlace work around the top and bottom of the grips. The wide flat pommels were usually covered with a plate of brass, silver or pewter that served as a washer for the fastening of the blade tang. This latter was usually a flat nut. The haunches seem to have been of unequal size and to have terminated in a crescent at the base of the blade much in the manner of the ballock knife. By about 1700 all-metal hilts made of brass or pewter had come into use, as had hilts with wood or bone grips and metal pommels and haunches (Plate 69). One scabbard datable to the seventeenth century survives. It belongs to the 1680 dirk mentioned above and is made of leather without metal mounts. The scabbard in the 1670 portrait, on the other hand, seems to be of dark leather with gilt locket and tip and a pocket for cutlery or implements on the front.

The first half of the eighteenth century saw the Scottish dirk reach the height of its development from both an aesthetic and a functional point of view. This was a fine weapon, well balanced, and designed for use as well as ornament. In normal practice the dirk of this period seems to have been held with the blade below the hand and used primarily as a stabbing weapon. When both broadsword and target were used, contemporary pictures indicate that the dirk was held in the left hand with its blade protruding below the edge of the shield. The average length of the dirks of this era was 18 ins., so that they were amply long to be so employed. Grips were short, but the thumb and forefinger encircled the expanding base of the pommel while the little finger curled about the juncture of the grip and haunches. With this grip the hilt was seized with the longest fingers around the greatest diameter and the shortest around the smallest part for a very satisfactory hold.

In appearance, the grips and haunches of the fully developed dirk were usually completely covered with vigorous interlace carving and, after 1750, sometimes studded with tiny nails or tacks. They were normally made of dark wood such as heather root. Metal and bone became less and less common as the century wore on. The pommel was fluted on its underside. The top was covered with a thick metal plate, usually brass, pewter or silver, though one gold-mounted piece is recorded in James Drummond's *Ancient Scottish Weapons* (Edinburgh and London, 1881). This plate was often engraved or pierced on the top with Celtic designs. The tang fastener remained an ornamental flat nut or, after *c.* 1740, often a knob. The haunches were normally bound at the bottom with a plate of the same metal as the pommel-cap, sometimes with bands running up the sides of the haunches. Blades continued to be evenly tapered and single-edged for most of their length, with a false edge or at least a bevel near the point. Now, however, they were often finely fluted on their flat faces, and sometimes they were pierced with simple circular holes. The backs might also be fluted or notched. Sometimes they were made from cut-down sword blades, and in these instances both the shapes and the flutings might differ. The edge of the blade normally retained its straight line from hilt to point, but the back would vary. Often the back followed the line of the old sword if it had been a back-sword, then turned at a slight angle and continued in a straight line to the point. Normally this angle marked the beginning of the false edge. The fullers were those of the old sword, and so they ran according to the axis of the original blade. Often there was only one at the back. Scabbards were usually made of dark leather with metal lockets and chapes (Plate 70). The mouth was shaped at the top to fit the crescent of the hilt haunches, and its lower border was often cut in decorative scrolls. In such instances the top of the chape was also cut in a matching pattern. As a rule there were two pockets, one above the other, for a small knife and a fork. In rare examples there were three pockets, two above and one below. Suspension was provided by a loop of leather and a 'D' ring or by separate rings sewed directly to the back of the sheath and provided with short chains, for the dirk normally hung from the girdle at the front of the wearer, much like some of the ancient ballock knives.

The fully developed dirk may have appeared early in the first quarter of the eighteenth century. Certainly, it had reached its peak between 1725 and 1750, and it continued to be made throughout the third quarter although more decadent forms had also appeared by that time. Even the Disarming Acts of 1716, 1725, and 1746 that followed various Scottish uprisings seem to have had little effect upon the dirk, except to make more sword blades available for cutting up into knives. The dirk, after all, did have a civilian function as a general utility knife, and it could be easily concealed. Also both privates and officers in the various Highland regiments wore the dirk as a prominent though unofficial part of their armament.

The decadence that afflicted the Scottish dirk set in gradually after 1750, and then gained momentum with the revival of Highland dress, following the repeal of prohibitions against such dress in 1782. This degeneration was marked by an exaggeration or attenuation of the main features of the hilt. The pommel became deeper and the grips thickened to a chunky appearance. The haunches became deeper, and there was a sharp line of demarcation between grips and haunches that had not existed previously when the two tended to blend together. At the same time, the crescentic lower edge of the haunches disappeared, and the line became straight, often with a pronounced lip. Decoration also deteriorated. The interlacings became broader and inferior in carving. In some dirks they were grotesquely bulbous; in others they were flat and indecisively carved, and in the final stages the interlacings became mere basketwork. In another, though less common, form of the degenerate hilt the features were shrivelled and small instead of exaggerated.

There was still a third design, influenced by the growing admiration for Classicism that characterized the period. This was the baluster-shaped grip, a form entirely new to Scottish weapons (Plate 71). The baluster had definitely appeared by the end of the third quarter of the century, and it became increasingly popular as the years passed, eventually developing into a thistle form shortly before 1800. Both the baluster and the thistle were completely impractical if the dirk was still being held in the traditional fashion with the blade below the hand, for it placed the thinnest portion of the grip where it would be seized with the longest fingers and the thickest portion in the area of the little finger. By this time, however, the target had disappeared from use as a fighting defence, and it is possible that the dirk was held with the blade above the hand if, indeed, it was really used for fighting at all. Privates in Highland regiments had ceased to carry it, and there were no more Scottish risings.

Blades varied little from the previous period, though in some the quality had noticeably deteriorated. Cut-down sword blades remained common. Scabbards continued in the same general form, but the metal mounts actually improved in quality. The cut-outs and piercings became finer, and engraved designs with Classical motifs came into use. It is possible also that the all-metal sheath, which became fashionable after 1800, also made its appearance before the turn of the century.

The Scottish dirk continued in great popularity during the nineteenth century, but it was no longer a fighting weapon in any real sense, even though officers of the Scottish regiments carried it. It had become an ornament of Highland costume, and as such it continues to be worn today. Silver was the popular metal for hilt mounts, and these mountings became heavier and heavier. Grips assumed an exaggerated thistle shape, carved with unimaginative basketwork (Plate 72). Finally pommels grew to great size, frequently mounted with a cairngorm, a plain crystal or an imitation in glass. Sometimes these pommels were tilted sideways so that the stone faced outwards instead of upwards. In some instances the tang of the blade no longer passed through the hilt, but was held in place by some sort of cement; in others it was secured by a nut under the pommel. Blades were poorly forged and became coventionalized with one narrow groove at the back and a broad shallow one in the centre. Metal scabbards became more common, though they were always rare, and after 1790 a spoon was occasionally added to the customary little knife and fork.

The Scottish dirk has had a long history from the middle of the seventeenth century until the present day. The eighteenth century, however, saw it reach its height as a weapon and as an object of art. Its later history belongs more to costume jewellery than to daggers and fighting knives, though there are records of dirks actually being used by officers and pipers in India during the nineteenth century.

Mediterranean Dirks and Peasant Knives

While the Scottish dirk was developing an entirely different form of dirk took shape in the territory bordering the Mediterranean Sea from Spain, along the southern coast of France to the Italian peninsula, and including the island of Sardinia. Like the Scottish dirk this form probably first appeared during the latter half of the seventeenth century, achieved its greatest development during the eighteenth century and continued through a good part, if not all, of the nineteenth. Unlike the Scottish weapon, which was remarkably uniform in its general appearance and construction, the Mediterranean dirk was made in a tremendous variety of shapes, styles, and forms of decoration.

There were, however, certain characteristics which permit these southern dirks to be recognized immediately once the collector becomes familiar with them. The handle is made in one piece (Plate 73). It is pierced for the tang of the blade, and there is no distinct pommel, although a silver cap sometimes overlays the butt-end. There is also no guard. Occasionally the base of the blade is cut out to form two projections that somewhat resemble vestigial quillons, but even this is extremely rare (Plate 75). Normally the handle terminates in a ferrule where it joins the ricasso, and it is this ricasso which offers one of the most salient features of the Mediterranean dirk. It is columnar in form, sometimes baluster in shape, sometimes baroque, faceted or floriate. On single-edged dirks it stems from the back of the blade; on double-eged types it arises from the centre of the blade.

The blades, too, are quite characteristic. The single-edged variety normally have a deep choil like a French chef's knife set at a sharp angle to the edge. Occasionally, however, the line of the choil is rounded instead of angular. The double-edged versions, on the other hand, normally have rounded shoulders at the base of the blade, and angular ones are rare. The lines of the back and edge sometimes taper towards each other in straight lines, but most often there is a slight convexity to the taper. The single-edged dirks usually also have a false edge for several inches from the point. On the better specimens the base of the blade is highly decorated with chiselling in low relief, piercings or engraved ornament, and sometimes with combinations of all three. Etching, blueing, and gilding, however, are rare.

The handles offer even more of a variety in form and decoration than the blades. In the earliest and finest specimens these are often made of horn, ivory or some close-grained wood like box and carved to represent single human figures or groups of figures. Most such finely carved handles are found on dirks attributed to southern France, and those specimens which bear dates were mostly made in the early eighteenth century. Other handles frequently encountered are made of ebony or horn and inlaid with silver or mother of pearl (Plate 75). Some are round in section and some octagonal, while others are fluted. Usually they swell slightly towards the end away from the blade and terminate in a rounded butt or a slight bird's shape. A late and very simple form of handle is made of light greenish cow horn carved with narrow flutes or reeds. Occasionally one also encounters metal handles and sometimes a form in which the outlines of the grips are composed merely of a framework of bars enclosing free rolling balls of bone, horn or metal. These are a few of the more common handle forms, but there are many more, for the makers seem to have been bound only by their own ingenuity and the the desires of their customers.

Surviving scabbards indicate that they were normally made of leather with metal throats and tips. For some reason, most of the sheaths that remain are quite plain with decoration confined to shaping the borders of the metal mounts and occasional light engraving. Yet it is entirely probable that there were also more elaborate sheaths with pierced and heavily engraved mounts to match the decoration of the blade. None of the scabbards show any provision for suspension, and so it is presumed that these knives were customarily thrust through the belt or sash and held in place by friction.

For many years collectors and students have termed these Mediterranean dirks 'peasant knives', and it is true that their appearance and such associations as are known indicate a popularity among the countryfolk rather than the more sophisticated city dwellers. The quality of the workmanship and decoration found on a large number of specimens, however, would seem to indicate that they were the weapons or ornaments of the landed gentry as well as the peasant (Plate 76).

American Scalping or Rifleman's Knives

The knife carried by the American frontier rifleman was very different from the finely made daggers of Europe. Yet it was just as useful a weapon, and it probably held a more important position in the armament of the man who carried it than any other knife of its day. The average European, after all, lived in a civilized area where knife combat was rare even in time of war. The American frontiersman lived daily in the shadow of attack from Indian warriors or wild beasts. He needed a good knife to protect himself in hand-to-hand combat once his rifle had been fired. He also needed a knife for general work in the woods. To meet these requirements a single knife had to be sturdy and large enough to serve as a weapon, yet not so big that it was unwieldy for camp duties. Because the frontiersman had few manufacturing facilities and little money to expend on ornamentation, his knife was usually simple, the blade forged by a local blacksmith or ground out of an old file and the haft a simple piece of wood or antler.

Actually very little is known about the knives carried by the American rifleman of the eighteenth century. Simply made specimens differ little from century to century, and so it is difficult to distinguish a crudely made eighteenth century knife from one made a hundred years later under similar conditions. There are no known dated specimens, and only one excavated blade that can clearly be documented as coming from this period, though one or two other knives survive that can reasonably be assumed to be of eighteenth-century origin. Written evidence also is scanty and unspecific. The city dwellers who saw riflemen pass through their communities on their way to join the newly formed American Army in 1775 spoke of the 'scalping' or 'butcher' knives in their belts. They mentioned also that every man carried one, but that is all the description they gave.

Despite this paucity of evidence, it is possible to conclude that there were actually two types of knife in common use by American frontiersmen. One was a simple quillon dagger, roughly forged with a double-edged blade and a short guard (Plate 77). The grip was a cylinder of wood pierced by the tang, which was slender, and driven into the wood until it held fast by friction. Sometimes a ferrule or two of iron, brass or pewter were added for extra strength. There was no pommel. Scabbards were of harness leather or rawhide without metal mounts, hand sewn and shaped to fit the blade.

The second form of knife was purely and simply a butcher knife, just as the contemporary documents seem to suggest. Judging from the number of accounts which use this descriptive term, it was probably the more common of the two forms of knife. The one excavated and clearly datable blade represents just this type (Plate 78). It was found in the parapet of an earthwork erected by American troops near Fort Ticonderoga in 1777 in such a position that it could only have got there when the work was being built. It is a single-edged blade with a very slightly curved back and an edge that curves from the short choil all the way to the point. The tang is narrow, and it is not in a direct line with the back, but slightly towards the centre of the blade. A few fragments of the original wooden handle still remain. This handle was obviously a simple cylinder of wood without a ferrule, but in other instances antler was quite probably used as well (Plate 79). The scabbard would have been similar to that described for the dagger.

Such knives as these were carried thrust through the belt, not suspended from it. Normally they were worn on an angle at the right front with the point towards the left and the handle to the right. At times they might be slipped farther around to the side, but they were kept far enough front so that they did not interfere with the powder horn or hunting bag which hung under the right arm.

Both types of knife seem to have developed early in the eighteenth century as settlers pushed westward into the Appalachians. They remained in use through the opening years of the nineteenth century, but gradually began to give way to more sophisticated knives imported from England or made by cutlers on the Eastern Seaboard. When the frontier moved beyond the Mississippi River they disappeared completely.

The rifleman's knife was the latest of the three principal eighteenth-century types to appear. It was also the first to vanish. The Mediterranean dirk lasted through much of the nineteenth century. The Scottish dirk persists to this day, but all reached the height of their development in the eighteenth century. Their later history was anticlimax.

80. Folding knife of the late eighteenth century large enough to have been used for fighting. The *navaja* was generally similar but had a handle that was slightly curved and that tapered to a point. *Richard Lennington Collection*

81. English folding pocket dagger of the mid nineteenth century. It belonged to John Wilkes Booth, assassin of President Abraham Lincoln. *U.S. National Park Service*

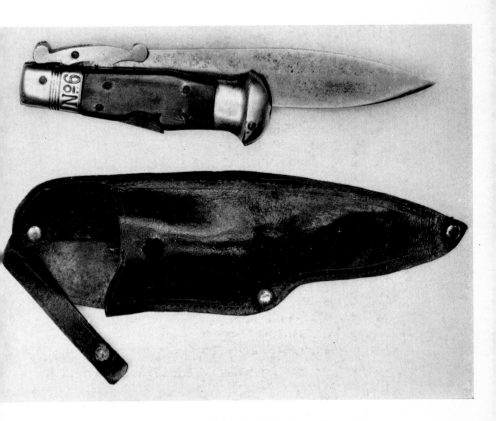

82. English folding dagger and sheath of the late nineteenth century. *Leon C. Jackson Collection*

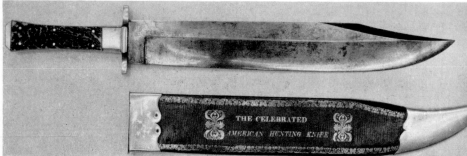

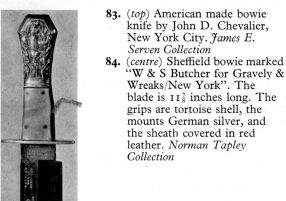

83. (*top*) American made bowie knife by John D. Chevalier, New York City. *James E. Serven Collection*

84. (*centre*) Sheffield bowie marked "W & S Butcher for Gravely & Wreaks/New York". The blade is 11⅞ inches long. The grips are tortoise shell, the mounts German silver, and the sheath covered in red leather. *Norman Tapley Collection*

85. (*left*) Sheffield bowie with horn grips and an alligator embossed on the German silver pommel. The blade is marked "Garrick/works/Sheffield" along with such phrases as "The Hunters Companion". This knife was used by Lewis Payne to stab Secretary of State Seward the night of Lincoln's assassination. *Dr. John K. Lattimer Collection*

86. (*right*) Sheffield bowie with spear point and horse head pommel. The mounts are German silver. *Courtesy, Ben Palmer*

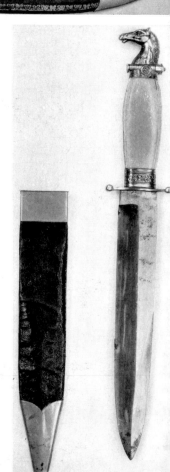

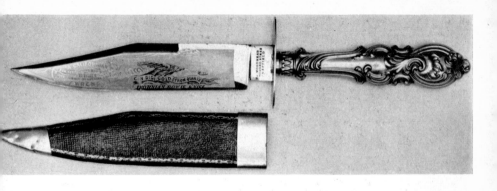

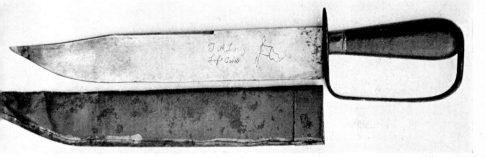

87. (*top*) Sheffield bowie with table cutlery handle and etched blade made by G. Woodhead. *Herb Glass Collection*

88. Confederate bowie with iron knuckle-bow and tinned iron sheath. *John D. Hammer Collection*

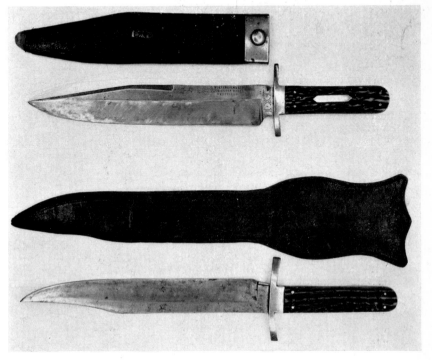

89. Sheffield bowie by George Wostenholm carried by a Union soldier during the Civil War. The grips are antler, and the knife is typical of the later and simpler bowie knives. *Courtesy, William Shemerluk*

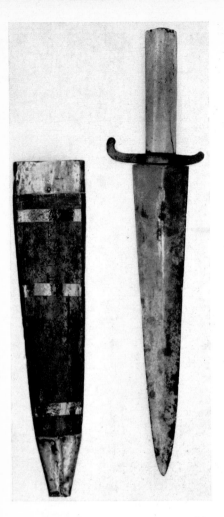

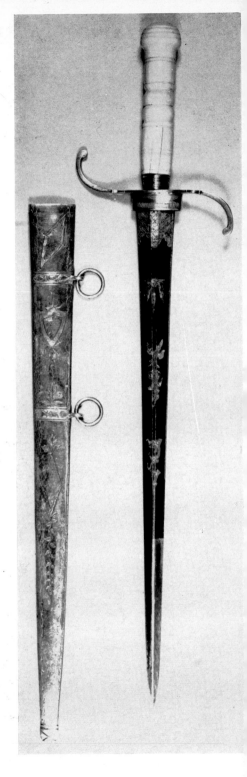

90. American dagger of the mid nineteenth century. The grip is bone, the mountings of the scabbard are brass. The iron guard has been put on upside down. *Courtesy, Ben Palmer*

91. American silver mounted dagger with ivory grip and blued and gilded blade of European origin, *c.* 1820. *Archer L. Jackson Collection*

92. American silver mounted dagger possibly carried by an army officer, *c.* 1810–20. *Dr. John K. Lattimer Collection*

93. American silver mounted dagger, *c.* 1820. *Dr. John K. Lattimer Collection*

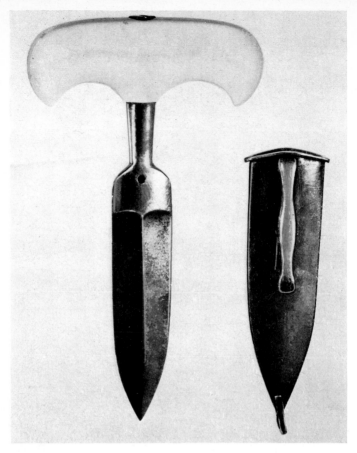

94. Push dagger of the type popular in the American South and West in the 1850s and 1860s. This specimen was made by Will & Fink, San Francisco. *United States National Museum, Washington*

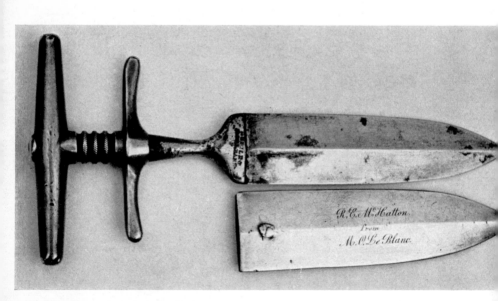

95. Push dagger with unusual double cross pieces made by Dufilho of New Orleans. *John D. Hammer Collection*

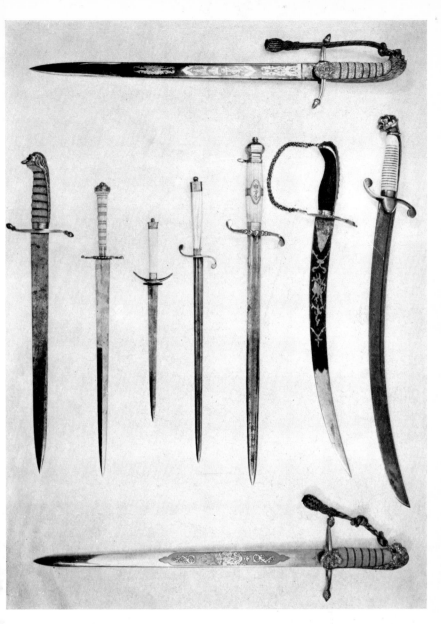

96–104. British naval dirks. Left to right: (1) midshipman's dirk of 1856 with white fish-skin grip and lion head pommel; (2) volunteer's dirk of about 1846 with ivory grips and a lion head pommel; (3) short dirk with the quillons in the form of the crown and flukes of an anchor, *c.* 1800–10; (4) light dirk with grooved blade, *c.* 1800–10; (5) five-ball type dirk with so-called pillow pommel and crown and anchor badge, 1790–1810; (6) dirk with blued and gilded blade and lion head pommel, *c.* 1810–20; (7) dirk or short hanger with lion head pommel, *c.* 1800. *Top:* Midshipman's dirk of 1878, as fitted with the lengthened blade, blued and gilt. *Bottom:* Midshipman's dirk of the pattern adopted in 1891 with an etched blade. This specimen bears the Tudor crown of 1901 in the badge. *National Maritime Museum, Greenwich*

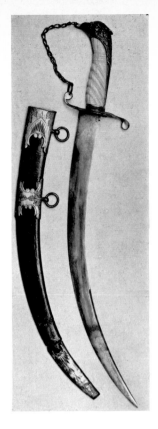

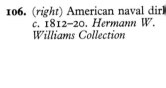

105. (*left*) American naval dirk
Capt. Stephen Decatur,
c. 1800–5. The grip is ivor
the mounts and scabbard,
brass. *U.S. Naval Academ
Museum, Annapolis*

106. (*right*) American naval dir
c. 1812–20. *Hermann W.
Williams Collection*

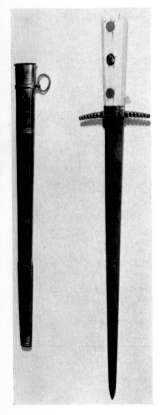

107. (*left*) American naval dirk
Capt. John Downes, *c.* 18
*U.S. Naval Academy Mus
Annapolis*

108. (*right*) American naval dir
the pattern of 1869. *U.S.
Naval Academy Museum,
Annapolis*

Chapter Six

The Nineteenth Century

Several factors influenced the history of daggers and fighting knives during the nineteenth century, but perhaps one of the most important was the growing industrial revolution. Water-power had been used for tilt-hammers and grinding wheels for centuries, but the early years of the nineteenth century witnessed the increasing use of such mechanized tools. Water-driven buffers joined an increasing array of grinders. Drop-forges for bolsters, guards and pommels became common, as did other mechanical aids. Increased precision in manufacture brought true assembly-line production to the field of knife manufacture and standard mass-produced models became increasingly common. The 'custom made' knife continued to be manufactured throughout the century, but by the 1890s it was hard-pressed by the standardized commercial product. Small local cutlers continued to make knives in all countries, but the wares of such big cutlery centres as Sheffield and Solingen found ever-widening markets throughout the Western world.

During the nineteenth century the knife and dagger continued to decline in importance until they reached their nadir in the 1880s and 1890s. The Scottish and Mediterranean dirks were made and worn through most of the period, but they were appurtenances of native costume rather than weapons. Naval dirks appeared and gained in popularity, especially during the first half of the century, but again they were more emblems of rank than weapons, and even they had fallen largely into disuse by 1900. Folding knives designed for fighting became popular among the gipsies, working people and sailors of Spain and Portugal between 1800 and 1850, but these were comparatively few in number and of little importance. The idea of military knives as weapons for private soldiers was still almost unexplored.

The one major exception to the general lack of interest in the knife as a weapon was found in America, especially in the southern and western states. There, men of all walks of life, law-abiding as well as criminal, were accustomed to wear a knife as a necessary part of their garb. Congressmen and senators even carried them into the United States Capitol. These were not mere decorations. The men who wore them did so for a purpose. It was a violent era, and a man might need a weapon at a moment's notice. The small pistol and the knife answered such a need, and so they were widely popular. This situation seems to have developed especially in the late 1820s and gained in momentum as the sectional strife which led to the American Civil War bred increased personal as well as political hostilities. The climax came in the 1850s. Then the war itself followed, and in the succeeding calm the practice of carrying knives gradually ceased, even in the West. While the period of conflict lasted this was the climate that produced the bowie knife, and the push dagger as well as countless other unnamed knives, but these, too, had all disappeared well before 1900. They mark the last appearance of the fighting knife and dagger as prominent civilian weapons before the forces of law and order and general decorum triumphed over personal violence.

Folding Knives

As noted above, the folding knife, known in Spain as the *navaja,* was the weapon of the gipsy, the peasant, the labourer and the sailor. It could be a tool, but it was also considered a weapon. At least one guide to the technique of wielding this knife was published in Madrid in 1849 and called *Manuel del Baratero ō Arte de Manejar la Navaja el Cuchillo y la Tijera de los Jitanos.* As the title indicates, it dealt not only with the *navaja,* but also the fixed-bladed knife and even scissors as gipsy weapons. Spaniards of the lower classes were evidently resourceful in their choice of arms.

As judged by surviving examples, the *navaja* varied considerably in size. It was always a single-bladed weapon, but that blade varied from 3 or 4 ins. in length to a full foot and sometimes even more. Perhaps the average length of a good-sized *navaja* blade was 6 to 8 ins. Despite their low origin and purpose, the steel of the blade was usually good and well tempered. The blade was locked in its open position by a spring catch. To release it, it was usually necessary to pull up on a ring, chain or flange provided for the purpose and so free the nose of the catch. The blade was then loose and could be returned to its closed position. Other *navaja* blades acted against a spring in the manner of a modern jack knife. The back of the blade was normally straight or slightly convex. The edge started parallel to the back, then curved up to meet it at the point.

The handles of the *navaja* were usually made of cow horn with iron linings. They curved in the direction of the edge of the blade and tapered from the hinge end to the tip that housed the point of the blade. As peasant and labourers' weapons they were normally completely plain and undecorated.

As is often the case with such simple weapons, no one knows exactly when they originated or when they ceased to be carried. Some specimens are known which may date from the eighteenth century, but it is difficult to be certain. The manual mentioned above gives one firm date for their use at mid-century and indicates by its comments that such knives had been popular for many years by that ime. The *navaja* may well have continued in use until 1900 or later, at least in remote parts of the Iberian Peninsula, but it certainly had lost its popularity well before that time. Thus one may safely assume that this was primarily a nineteenth-century knife, though it probably had its origins in the eighteenth century.[1]

The *navaja* was not the only large clasp knife that could be used for a weapon. Elsewhere in Europe big folding knives appeared, and though there are no other manuals or specific references to their use as weapons, their very size indicates that this was their purpose (Plate 80). After all, a knife with a 10- or 12-in. blade is too big for the normal uses of a pocket or pen knife. These large folding knives are often indistinguishable from the *navaja* except that the special spring catch for the blade and its release ring are seldom encountered outside the Iberian Peninsula and near-by northern Africa. Also brass or iron bolsters that add strength to the pivot of the blade seem to be more common outside the area of the *navaja*. These big single-bladed knives that are so closely allied to the *navaja* were definitely made at least as early as the second half of the eighteenth century, for dated and associated specimens are known, and this is one more reason for assigning such a date to the *navaja* as well. Unlike the *navaja*,

[1] See also the note on p. 80.

however, these big knives seem to have disappeared early in the nineteenth century as far as the rest of Europe was concerned.

The idea of a folding weapon did not disappear, however. In the middle and late nineteenth century a small group of folding knives appeared that came to be known as folding dirks, folding daggers or pocket daggers. Both Sheffield and Solingen produced them in some quantity and variety. Some were designed to be carried in the pocket with blades that were no longer than the hilt, so that they could be safely folded up with the edge and point covered (Plate 81). Others were so long that even when folded the blade projected (Plate 82). One especially long specimen survives with a blade 16¾ ins. long when extended and 10 ins. long when closed. It is so designed that it can be used either open or closed, depending upon the length of the blade the user felt desirable for the circumstances. Such a knife necessarily required a scabbard. Most, but not all, of these folding daggers boasted simple cross quillons, but a few had only a bolster. Blades might be double- or single-edged, and the handles assumed a variety of forms, but always there was a bolster at the pivot and usually a pommel at the other end.

The extent to which folding daggers were used in Europe is unknown. It seems unlikely that they found a big market in either England or Germany, where they were made. Rather, America seems to have been the intended sales area. The decoration on surviving specimens often includes the eagle and other American motifs. John Wilkes Booth, the assassin of President Abraham Lincoln in 1865, had a Sheffield-made folding dagger in his pocket when he was killed by pursuing soldiers after the tragedy, and sufficient examples of the genre are found in the United States to indicate this country as the primary market.

Bowie Knives

Few knives of recent years have captured the imagination as thoroughly as the bowie knife. It immediately conjures up a picture of a rough and ready environment with violence an ever-present threat. This is just as true of the time when the knife was actually used as it is today. Visitors to the United States from Europe were awed by the huge knife and felt constrained to comment about it at length in their writings. Citizens from the north-eastern part of the country felt the same reaction when they

ventured south or west into the area of the bowie knife's domination. Even in its own domain, state legislatures in Tennessee,
Alabama, and Mississippi passed laws covering the use, transfer,
or even public handling of the dread weapon in an attempt to
minimize what they considered its violent influence.

The history of the bowie knife begins in 1827. In that year the
famous American frontiersman and soldier, James Bowie (1795-
1836), was given a knife by his brother Rezin. Little is known
about this weapon except that it had a straight, single-edged blade
$9\frac{1}{4}$ ins. long and $1\frac{1}{2}$ ins. wide and had been designed by Rezin himself for use in hunting. Jim Bowie used the knife in several adven-
tures and became very attached to it as a weapon. Then, in 1830, he is
reputed to have asked an Arkansas blacksmith named James
Black to make him an improved version of it. There is little
support for this tale save Black's own testimony given many years
later when the knife had become famous—and even he did not
indicate the nature of the improvements. Possibly they included
adding a false edge at the point and, just possibly, the introduction
of the clipped point in which the back swoops to meet the edge
in a concave line.

Whatever the design of the original bowie knife, its fame
spread rapidly across the land. Bowie's exploits in knife-fighting,
and his heroic death at the Alamo in 1836 attracted tremendous
attention. People everywhere wanted a knife like Bowie's—even
if they did not know exactly what that weapon looked like. They
did know that it was a big all-purpose fighting knife stout to
attack another human, split a bear's skull, lop off a sapling with a
single blow or dig in hard ground. They generally agreed that it
was single-edged, but beyond that no one seemed to care. All big
single-edged fighting knives soon came to be called bowie knives.

The first of these bowie knives were made by American smiths
in the old Southwest—Mississippi, Arkansas, Louisiana, and
Texas, and possibly also in Tennessee and Missouri (Plate 83).
Blades ranged in length on an average from 9 to 15 ins., and they
might be $1\frac{1}{2}$-2 ins. wide. They were often well made, but lacked
the high finish of later imported models. Guards usually consisted
of simple quillons, sometimes bent in an S curve, or else just a
plate of brass or iron. Grips were commonly wood, antler, or
bone, and they might be made in either one or two pieces. Normally there were no inscriptions, or decorations though a few of the

better cutlers, such as Searles of Baton Rouge, might mark their products. On a few of the early blacksmith-made specimens there was another interesting feature. This was a strip of hardened brass fastened along the back of the blade and usually keyed both to the blade and the cross guard. Supposedly this strip was designed to catch the edge of an opponent's knife and prevent it from slipping off in a parry. Knives with original strips of brass are extremely rare today, and the addition of such strips to later knives has proved a great temptation to forgers. Collectors should remember that these strips are found only on the big American-made specimens, never on English imports, and that they are attached mechanically to the blade, not simply soldered or sweated in place.

Within a very few years of the appearance of the early American bowie knives, English products began to reach the American market. George Wostenholm, founder of the Washington Works in Sheffield, had a representative in America as early as 1830, and he personally made visits in 1836 and later to study the market for knives. Wostenholm probably made more and better bowies than any other English firm. His trademark of **I*XL** became so much of a standard that other companies began to imitate it with such variants as **XLNT, I*XCD, NON*XL,** and the like. Ranging behind Wostenholm came such other Sheffield firms as Joseph Rodgers & Sons, Edward Barnes, and Alexander, and behind these came a whole host of others. Some tried to enhance the American appeal of their products by marking blades and scabbards with the letters **US** separated by a star or **NY** separated by a federal shield. None, however, had any official connexion with the United States Government or the State of New York. The marks were purely decorative and suggestive.

It was with these English imports that the great variety of form characterizing the secondary bowies first began to appear. Some of them followed the classical form with large blades and clipped points. Most, however, offered the spear point which was symmetrical in its conformation with both the true edge and the false edge coming together in convex curves. Still others introduced the slanted point with the back angling to meet the edge in a straight line. Blades ran all the way from 6 to 14 or 15 ins. At the same time, the false edge changed in character. Whereas it had almost always been sharpened in the American forms, it was often a simple swage or bevel in the English versions and not functional at all.

Bowie-knife hilts also increased in variety with the appearance of the English-made specimens (Plate 85). White brass, German silver, sterling, and coin silver joined brass and iron as metals for mounts. Usually, these mounts consisted of a guard, a ferrule at the base of the grips, sometimes an escutcheon plate on one side of the grips, and often a cap or pommel at the butt end of the hilt. Grips might be made of one or two pieces of wood, bone, ivory, mother-of-pearl, horn, antler, tortoise shell, silver, or German silver.

Blade decoration also reached new heights. Generally these enrichments were acid etched on the metal and left bright. In a few instances, however, blueing and gilding were used to enhance the etching, and in later types a gilt background was sometimes employed to accent the bright unetched areas. Most of these decorations involved the use of patriotic or jingoistic slogans designed to capture the fancy of American buyers, but there were also references to the search for gold after 1849 and, still later, mottoes related to the conflict over slavery, such as 'Death to Abolition' or 'Death to Traitors'. Some knives simply identified themselves as 'A Sure Defence' or the 'Self Protector', 'The American Hunting Knife' or 'The Genuine Arkansas Toothpick'. In addition to these etched designs, there were also a large number of simple stampings that included pictures of sphinxes, mounted hunters, dogs, deer, lions, unicorns, and the like with such words as 'Try Me', 'The Hunter's Companion', 'Alabama Hunting Knife', and references to General Zachary Taylor's victory at Buena Vista in the Mexican War.

Hilts also were decorated in a variety of fashions. One of the most popular designs was copied from the table cutlery of the era with scrollwork and shells (Plate 87). These hilts were usually made of German silver or of true silver, but gutta-percha was also employed. There were pommels shaped like horses' heads or shells as well as representations of the legendary half-horse half-alligator symbol of the backwoods rifleman (Plate 87). Sometimes, too, there were state crests, especially the Louisiana pelican with its young, patriotic motifs such as eagles, flags, federal shields, and the word 'Liberty'.

Bowie knife scabbards varied according to whether they were

made in England or America. Sheffield specimens were normally constructed of pressed paper or cardboard with a thin veneer of coloured leather. They were handsome sheaths in red, yellow, green, blue, purple or brown, among other colours, and normally there was also some gilt tooling in the form of a decorative border and sometimes a stamped central design as well. There were also metal mounts in the form of a locket with a stud and a tip or chape. The locket was a relatively narrow band, occasionally with scalloped edges, but more often straight. The tip followed the contour of the knife point. German silver was the most popular for these mounts, but for very fancy specimens real silver might also be used. American scabbards in general followed the same design as the English products, but they were normally made of black harness-leather, which was much stouter than the English construction. Some American scabbards had no metal mounts at all, and those that did offered a greater variety of metals, including brass, iron and tinned iron as well as silver and German silver. Some American scabbards had studs on the throat so that the knife could be thrust through the belt in the traditional fashion with the stud serving to hold it in place. Other American sheaths, however, are equipped with belt-loops or even complete frogs for suspension. Since the English scabbards of pressed paper were so flimsy that they usually disintegrated after a short period of hard use, many Sheffield bowies are found today with American sheaths made by some local saddler or cobbler to replace the original. In such instances, even the original metal mounts have failed to survive, because the new leather was so much thicker that they could not be made to fit.

The American Civil War marked the turning-point in the history of the bowie knife. At the outset the big knife was a popular weapon on both sides (Plate 89). Confederate troops especially prized it, and many big knives with knuckle guards were produced for the war (Plate 88). Some of these were actually short-swords, though the records continued to call them bowies or side knives. By the end of the conflict men of both armies had largely abandoned such arms as superfluous, and the era of peace and easing tensions which followed saw the custom of wearing knives decline sharply. Buffalo hunters and cowboys and some other westerners carried big knives for a while, but these became more and more hunting knives rather than weapons. Their size diminished, and their handles soon began to sport grips made of hard rubber or various synthetic materials. By 1880 the true bowie knife had vanished.

American Daggers

Side by side with the bowie another series of knives developed in America that represented almost a throwback to the quillon daggers of the sixteenth century or at least a continuation of the rifleman's daggers a hundred years earlier (Plate 90). They boasted straight double-edged blades that tapered from hilt to point in either a straight or slightly convex line. Their guards were true quillons, sometimes straight, sometimes curved towards the blade and sometimes S-curved (Plate 91). The grips were normally, one piece, without a true pommel, and made of wood, antler bone, ivory or even silver. A number of these daggers are known mounted in silver and complete with silver scabbards, and their dates of origin appear to range from the 1790s until about 1830. Many have military motifs or associations, and it is presumed that they were worn by Army officers when they were off duty and did not wish to carry a sword (Plates 92 and 93). Fancy presentation daggers were also made as late as the 1860s.

Alongside the fine silver daggers and the presentation specimens there were also a large number of cruder specimens with big blades, heavy iron guards, and one-piece handles of wood or antler. Examples have been excavated at a number of fur trading-post sites of the early nineteenth century, and the type seems to have remained in use through much of the bowie period, though it was never as popular as the single-edged knife. Some students have tried to distinguish these daggers with the name Arkansas toothpick, a term which appears in contemporary documents. It appears, however, that this is an artificial distinction. Most early writers seem to have used the terms bowie knife and Arkansas toothpick synonymously, with the latter actually as a joking reference to the state that supposedly gave birth to the bowie knife.

There was also one final form of dagger that seems to have been unique to America and to the early nineteenth century. This was the so-called push dagger (Plates 94 and 95). It consisted of a short double-edged blade that sprang from a cylindrical stem. This stem, in turn, passed through a transverse handle, usually made of wood, bone, or ivory. The dagger was grasped with the stem passing between the second and third fingers, so that the blow would be delivered with a punching motion somewhat similar to that used with the Indian katar. Scabbards might be leather or metal, and frequently they were designed to be hung upside down under the wearer's jacket. A spring catch engaged a hole in the base of the blade to hold the knife in place and keep it from falling out, and a little hook at the tip of the scabbard privided for suspension. Surviving specimens of this form that can be dated all come from the 1848-60 period, and they seem to be associated with the South and West.

Naval Dirks

The naval dirk was a special weapon that seems first to have appeared in the late eighteenth century and gained its real period of popularity in the nineteenth century. At different periods midshipmen and naval cadets wore dirks as their only weapon, and at other times Regular officers up to and including flag rank wore them with their undress uniforms, sometimes both afloat and ashore, sometimes only afloat. New regulations appeared to change the situation every few years.

In Great Britain references to midshipmen wearing dirks date back at least to 1775, but in the regulations of 1805 swords were specifically listed for them and dirks were not mentioned. Probably they continued in use, however, for in 1825 midshipmen, volunteers (later naval cadets) and masters assistants were specifically forbidden to wear dirks. This was changed two years later, when dirks were ordered for volunteers, but the reinstitution was short-lived and they were again shelved in favour of swords in 1846. Ten years later the dirk returned in full force when midshipmen, naval cadets, and masters assistants lost their swords for good. Dirks remained in use for these groups through the rest of the century, and finally in 1936 even paymaster cadets who had never had any weapon were allowed to wear them.

Interestingly enough, although dirks are mentioned with some regularity in naval orders there are no illustrations or descriptions of them until 1856. Thus a great diversity of designs existed, and the student must attempt to assign dates to surviving specimens on the basis of their design and decoration or on their known association with a given individual (Plates 96-104). This naturally leaves room for considerable error, but certain general phases of evolution do seem to be identifiable. During the period before 1825 two main types of dirk seem to have been in general use. One was a straight double-edged weapon with a slender blade between 8 and 18 ins. long. Often it had a central fuller; at other times it was diamond-shaped in cross-section. Grips were normally ivory and of one piece, often rectangular in section and sometimes reeded. Pommels were sometimes simple caps, and at other times they resembled those on contemporary swords with faceted sides. This was especially true of one group of dirks that reflected the design of the contemporary five-ball swords (so-called because of the appearance of five balls as decoration on their knuckle bows and counter guards) and were generally much more substantial weapons than the usual dirk of the period. These five-ball dirks had a branch on the obverse side of their S-curved quillons decorated with the ball design as contrasted with the commoner dirk that boasted no such branch on its similarly curved guard. Early in the nineteenth century these light straight dirks were joined by another pattern with a stout curved blade 14-16 ins. long. These were single-edged weapons, flat-sided, and decorated with etching, blueing, and gilding for about two-thirds of their length. The hilts somewhat resembled those on contemporary swords. Grips were normally made of wood, bone, or ivory, and they were ribbed or grooved to offer a better hold. There was normally a ferrule at the base of the grips, a backstrap, and a pommel that might be either a simple cap or a lion's head. A chain connected the pommel with the quillons. At one time it was thought that these dirks dated as late as 1827, but it now seems more likely that they appeared as early as 1810 or 1812, when the same design became popular in America. Indeed, since American designs normally copied those of Great Britain or France, it is quite possible that these curved British dirks may be even earlier.

Between 1827 and 1846 the most popular dirk again seems to have been a straight double-edged weapon, but this time it was a slightly heavier arm, and the hilt was quite different. The primary material for the grips remained ivory, but they were usually turned with a series of ridges instead of being straight sided. The pommel also featured a lion head in low relief on the cap.

In 1856 the first specifically designated model of dirk became regulation. It was a stouter arm than any of the previous models except the five-ball and the curved types. The blade was straight, about 1⅛ ins. wide and 12 or 13 ins. long. It was single-edged, but there was a false edge near the point. In response to complaints from midshipmen who had to fight ashore with this weapon during the Indian Mutiny the blade was lengthened to 17¾ ins. about 1870. The grips were covered with white fish skin and bound with twisted wire like those on contemporary naval swords. There was a ferrule at the base of the grips and a backstrap that terminated in a lion-head pommel with a loop in its mouth for a sword knot. The quillons were slightly S-curved and terminated in acorn finials on both ends.

The pattern of 1856 remained the general standard for British naval dirks for the rest of the century. There were minor variations, of course. Some time in the 1870s blued and gilt decorations became standard for blades, but they disappeared and were replaced by bright etching against a frosted background about 1891. Plaques with wreath crown and anchors also appeared on the centre of the quillons where they crossed the blade in the 1870s and they remained standard at least for the rest of the century.

American dirks had a shorter history, but just as great a variety of designs as their British counterparts. The first recorded reference to dirks in the United States Navy appears in the regulations of 1802 with the statement that they were not to be worn on shore. This would seem to indicate that the dirk was already in use and that it had been for some time. Dirks are again mentioned in the regulations of 1813, when both officers and midshipmen were permitted to wear them with undress uniform. Then there is a hiatus of fifty-six years without any reference to the weapon in official orders or regulations, although there is considerable evidence that it continued to be a popular arm. In 1869 the silence is broken and an official model dirk described and illustrated. The dirk is mentioned again in the regulations of 1876, and then it drops completely from sight in official orders. There is no indication when the dirk was abandoned, but it probably disappeared within ten years of the 1876 regulation, and it was certainly gone before the turn of the century.

With no official dirk pattern before 1869, the choice of design was left to the taste of the individual officer, just as it had been in the British Navy. Nevertheless, certain general patterns predominated in various periods. The first American dirks were stout daggers with straight double-edged blades that tapered evenly from hilt to point (Plate 105). Usually they were a flat diamond-shape in cross-section. These blades might be 9 or 10 ins. long and perhaps 1½ ins. wide at the guard. This guard consisted of wide quillons normally made of gilded brass. There was usually a gilded brass ferrule at the base of the faceted bone or ivory grips and no pommel. Scabbards were either gilt brass or leather with gilt brass mounts.

Before 1810 these heavy straight dirks gave way to a curved version very like those popular with British naval officers (Plate 106). Even the popular length of from 14 to 16 ins. measured in a straight line from hilt to point was retained in the American versions. Instead of the British lion for a pommel, however, the American dirks boasted eagle heads and sometimes the gilt etched decorations of the blade featured American motifs. Otherwise they were almost identical weapons.

About 1820 the popularity of these curved dirks was dented by the reappearance of a straight-bladed dagger (Plate 107). It was considerably lighter than the earlier design, however, and normally it had an etched blade whereas the first pattern had always been plain. Hilts varied; some were made entirely of gilt brass, but most boasted small quillons or a circular counterguard of brass and one-piece ivory or bone grips. Some had no pommel whatsoever; some offered a knob made as part of the grips. By 1825 these straight dirks had completely superseded the curved pattern, and they are believed to have remained in use until the appearance of the first official pattern in 1869.

This 1869 model was a simple and somewhat crude arm (Plate 108). It was intended only for midshipmen, for officers were forebidden to carry dirks. It retained the straight double-edged blade of its predecessors. The quillons, however, became stouter and more functional, and they bore simple incised decorations. The grips were made of wood covered with white fish skin and wrapped with wire like those on contemporary naval officer's swords. The eagle head returned to the pommel, but it was a crude and ugly casting. The scabbard was made of black leather with plain brass mounts and two carrying rings for suspension. The regulations of 1876 mentioned the dirk, but do not describe it. Presumably it remained the same, so that it was this unlovely weapon which marked the end of the dirk in American naval history.

Other nations in addition to Great Britain and the United States also recognized the naval dirk. Denmark probably had the greatest variety of designs, but most seafaring countries saw at least a few worn by their naval officers and midshipmen. Interestingly enough, the story is largely the same everywhere. The regulations and orders are silent on design, so that it is necessary to date specimens by style and other secondary means. On the whole straight double-edged types have predominated with only a few curved patterns outside Great Britain and America. All were primarily products of the nineteenth century, and in most cases they fell from use before the century was over. Some, like the British, however, seem still to have been in use when the year 1900 brought an end to the era.

With the beginning of the nineteenth century the history of the dagger and fighting knife seems to have passed its nadir. Right at the outset trench knives were introduced by both sides during World War I, so that the common soldier was once again equipped with a knife designed primarily for combat. World War II brought an even greater variety of knife weapons for soldiers and marines. There were bowie types, stilettos, true daggers, and a host of other designs. Bayonets that could be also used as fighting knives reappeared in quantity for the first time since the seventeenth century, and even the dress dagger was revived in Germany, Italy, and their conquered territories during the 1930s and 1940s. So far has the pendulum swung that American astronauts now carry big all-purpose knives with fighting guards on their trips through space. Many collectors are already interested in these products of the twentieth century, even though it is still too early to know what the overall contribution of this hundred years will be. So far all signs seem to indicate that the history which began some 500,000 years ago still has a long way to go.

NOTE—Since the above was written the Editor has drawn my attention to two references to *The Navaja and its use in Spain* by Charles d'Avillier and Gustave Doré (London, 1881, pp. 85 and 213–5). Among other things the authors describe how they 'had the curiosity to take lessons from a professor [of fencing with the navaja], who disclosed the secrets of his science, aided by an ordinary cane in case of the bare blade'.

Select Bibliography

The literature of daggers and fighting knives is extensive if one considers all of the catalogues which include some examples of this type of weapon and all books and magazine articles which mention them or give hurried histories. The old *Zeitschrift für Historische Waffenkunde* alone offers hundreds of articles in which daggers are discussed. The following list attempts only to suggest writings that are especially useful to collectors because of their detailed treatment of broad aspects of the subject. It is intended primarily as a guide for further reading and for assistance in the identification of specimens.

Abels, Robert, *Classic Bowie Knives,* New York, 1967.

Blair, Claude, *European & American Arms,* London, 1962.

Blair, Claude, and John Wallace, 'Scots—or still English?' *Scottish Art Review,* IX, No. 1 (1963), 11-15, 34-37.

Bosson, Clement, 'Les Dagues Suisses', *Geneva,* XII (1964), 167-98.

Childe, V. Gordon, *The Bronze Age,* Cambridge, 1930.

Dean, Bashford, *Catalogue of European Daggers,* New York, 1929.

Jacobsen, Holger, 'Marinens Vagtdolke', *Vaabenhistoriske Aarbøger,* VII, (1952-4), 107-32.

Keener, William G., *Bowie Knives from the Collections of Robert Abels and the Ohio Historical Society,* Columbus, Ohio, 1962.

Laking, Sir Guy F., *A Record of European Armour and Arms through Seven Centuries,* 5 vols., London, 1920-22.

Mann, Sir James, *Wallace Collection Catalogues, European Arms and Armour,* 2 vols., London, 1962.

May, Commander W. E., and A. N. Kennard, *Naval Swords and Firearms,* London, 1962.

Norman, A. V. B., 'Early Military Dirks in the Scottish United Services Museum, Edinburgh', *Journal of the Arms and Armour Society,* IV, No. 1, (March 1962), 1-23.

Oakes, R. Ewart, *The Archaeology of Weapons,* London, 1960.

Peterson, Harold L., *American Knives,* New York, 1958.

Rodriguez Lorente, J. J., 'The XVth Century Ear Dagger. Its Hispano-Moresque Origin', *Gladius,* III (1964), 67-87.

Seitz, Heribert, *Blankwaffen,* 2 vols., Brunswick, 1965-7.

Terenzi, Marcello, *Considerazioni su di un tipo di pugnale detto Stiletto da Bombardiere,* Rome, 1962.

Ullmann, Konrad, 'Dolchmesser, Dolch und Kurzwehren des 15, und 16. Jahrhunderts in Kernraum der Hanse', *Waffen- und Kostümkunde,* Dritte Folge III (1961), 1-13, 114-27.

Wegeli, Rudolf, *Inventar der Waffensammlung des Bernsichen historischen Museums in Bern,* 4 vols., Berne, 1942-48. Volume II deals with daggers.

Whitelaw, Charles, 'The Origin and Development of the Highland Dirk', *The Transactions of the Glasgow Archaeological Society,* New Series, V (1908), 32-42.

Index